THE PASSING OF THE FRONTIER

THE YALE CHRONICLES
OF AMERICA SERIES

The Passing of the Frontier

A Chronicle
of the
Old West

by
Emerson Hough

1970

Toronto
Glasgow, Brook & Co.

New York
United States Publishers
Association, Inc.

CONTENTS

I.	THE FRONTIER IN HISTORY	Page	1
II.	THE RANGE	"	11
III.	THE CATTLE TRAILS	"	28
IV.	THE COWBOY	"	40
V.	THE MINES	"	57
VI.	PATHWAYS OF THE WEST	"	83
VII.	THE INDIAN WARS	"	112
VIII.	THE CATTLE KINGS	"	137
IX.	THE HOMESTEADER	"	151
	BIBLIOGRAPHICAL NOTE	"	175
	INDEX	"	179

THE PASSING OF THE FRONTIER

∴

CHAPTER I

THE FRONTIER IN HISTORY

THE frontier! There is no word in the English language more stirring, more intimate, or more beloved. It has in it all the *élan* of the old French phrase, *En avant!* It carries all of the old Saxon command, *Forward!* It means all that America ever meant. It means the old hope of a real personal liberty, and yet a real human advance in character and achievement. To a genuine American it is the dearest word in all the world.

What is, or was, the frontier? Where was it? Under what stars did it lie? Because, as the vague Iliads of ancient heroes or the nebulous records of the savage gentlemen of the Middle Ages make small specific impingement on our consciousness today, so also even now begin the

1

tales of our own old frontier to assume a haziness, an unreality, which makes them seem less history than folklore. Now the truth is that the American frontier of history has many a local habitation and many a name. And this is why it lies somewhat indefinite under the blue haze of the years, all the more alluring for its lack of definition, like some old mountain range, the softer and more beautiful for its own shadows.

The fascination of the frontier is and has ever been an undying thing. Adventure is the meat of the strong men who have built the world for those more timid. Adventure and the frontier are one and inseparable. They suggest strength, courage, hardihood — qualities beloved in men since the world began — qualities which are the very soul of the United States, itself an experiment, an adventure, a risk accepted. Take away all our history of political régimes, the story of the rise and fall of this or that partizan aggregation in our government; take away our somewhat inglorious military past; but leave us forever the tradition of the American frontier! There lies our comfort and our pride. There we never have failed. There, indeed, we always realized our ambitions. There, indeed, we were efficient, before that hateful phrase was known. There we were a melting-pot for character, before we came to know that odious appellation which classifies us as the melting-pot of the nations.

The frontier was the place and the time of the strong man, of the self-sufficient but restless individual. It was the home of the rebel, the protestant, the unreconciled, the intolerant, the ardent — and the resolute. It was not the conservative and tender man who made our history; it was the man sometimes illiterate, oftentimes uncultured, the man of coarse garb and rude weapons. But the frontiersmen were the true dreamers of the nation. They really were the possessors of a national vision. Not statesmen but riflemen and riders made America. The noblest conclusions of American history still rest upon premises which they laid.

But, in its broadest significance, the frontier knows no country. It lies also in other lands and in other times than our own. When and what was the Great Frontier? We need go back only to the time of Drake and the sea-dogs, the Elizabethan Age, when all North America was a frontier, almost wholly unknown, compellingly alluring to all bold men. That was the day of new stirrings in the human heart. Some strange impulse seemed to act upon the soul of the braver and bolder Europeans; and they moved westward, nor could have helped that had they tried. They lived largely and blithely, and died handsomely, those old Elizabethan adventurers, and they lie today in thousands of unrecorded graves upon two continents, each having found out that any place is good enough for a man to die upon, provided that he be a man.

The American frontier was Elizabethan in its quality — childlike, simple, and savage. It has not entirely passed; for both Elizabethan folk and Elizabethan customs are yet to be found in the United States. While the half-savage civilization of the farther West was roaring on its way across the continent — while the day of the keelboatman and the plainsman, of the Indian-fighter and the miner, even the day of the cowboy, was dawning and setting — there still was a frontier left far behind in the East, near the top of the mountain range which made the first great barrier across our pathway to the West. That frontier, the frontier of Boone and Kenton, of Robertson and Sevier, still exists and may be seen in the Cumberlands — the only remaining part of America which is all American. There we may find trace of the Elizabethan Age — idioms lost from English literature and American speech long ago. There we may see the American home life as it went on more than a hundred years ago. We may see hanging on the wall the long muzzle-loading rifle of an earlier day. We may see the spinning-wheel and the loom. The women still make in part the clothing for their families, and the men still make their own household furniture, their own farming implements, their own boots.

This overhanging frontier of America is a true survival of the days of Drake as well as of the days of Boone. The people are at once godly and savage. They breed freely; they love their homes; they are ever ready for adventure; they are frugal, abstemious, but violent and strong. They carry on still the half-religious blood feuds of the old Scotch Highlands or the North of Ireland, whence they came. They reverence good women. They care little for material accumulations. They believe in personal ease and personal independence. With them life goes on not in the slow monotony of reiterated performance, but in ragged profile, with large exertions followed by large repose. Now that has been the fashion of the

frontier in every age and every land of all the
world. And so, by studying these people, we
may even yet arrive at a just and comprehen-
sive notion of what we might call the "feel" of
the old frontier.

There exists, too, yet another Saxon frontier
in a far-off portion of the world. In that strange
country, Australia, tremendous unknown regions
still remain, and the wild pastoral life of such
regions bids fair to exist yet for many years. A
cattle king of Queensland held at one time sixty
thousand square miles of land. It is said that the
average size of pastoral holdings in the northern
territory of Australia is two hundred and seventy-
five thousand acres. Does this not recall the old
times of free range in the American West?

This strange antipodal civilization also retains
a curious flavor of Elizabethan ideas. It does not
plan for inordinate fortunes, the continual amass-
ing of money, but it does deliberately plan for
the use by the individual of his individual life.
Australian business hours are shorter than American. Routine is less general. The individual takes
upon himself a smaller load of effort. He is res-
tive under monotony. He sets aside a great part
of his life for sport. He lives in a large and young

day of the world. Here we may see a remote picture of our own American West — better, as it seems to me, than that reflected in the rapid and wholly commercialized development of Western Canada, which is not flavored by any age but this.

But much of the frontier of Australia is occupied by men of means who had behind them government aid and a semi-paternal encouragement in their adventures. The same is true in part of the government-fostered settlement of Western Canada. It was not so with the American West. Here was not the place of the rich man but of the poor man, and he had no one to aid him or encourage him. Perhaps no man ever understood the American West who did not himself go there and make his living in that country, as did the men who found it and held it first. Each life on our old frontier was a personal adventure. The individual had no government behind him and he lacked even the protection of any law.

Our frontier crawled west from the first seaport settlements, afoot, on horseback, in barges, or with slow wagon-trains. It crawled across the Alleghanies, down the great river valleys and up them yet again; and at last, in days of new transportation, it leaped across divides, from one river valley to another. Its history, at first so halting, came to be very swift — so swift that it worked great elisions in its own story.

In our own day, however, the Old West generally means the old cow country of the West — the high plains and the lower foothills running from the Rio Grande to the northern boundary. The still more ancient cattle-range of the lower Pacific Slope will never come into acceptance as the Old West. Always, when we use these words, we think of buffalo plains and of Indians, and of their passing before the footmen and riders who carried the phantom flag of Drake and the Virgin Queen from the Appalachians to the Rockies — before the men who eventually made good that glorious and vaunting vision of the Virginia cavaliers, whose party turned back from the Rockfish Gap after laying claim in the name of King George on all the country lying west of them, as far as the South Sea!

The American cow country may with very good logic arrogate to itself the title of the real and typical frontier of all the world. We call the spirit of the frontier Elizabethan, and so it was; but even as the Elizabethan Age was marked by its contact with the Spanish civilization in Europe, on the high seas, and in both the Americas, so the last frontier of the American West also was affected, and largely, deeply, by Spanish influence and Spanish customs. The very phraseology of range work bears proof of this. Scores of Spanish words are written indelibly in the language of the Plains. The frontier of the cow-range never was Saxon alone.

It is a curious fact also, seldom if ever noted, that this Old West of the Plains was very largely Southern and not Northern on its Saxon side. No States so much as Kentucky and Tennessee and, later, Missouri — daughters of Old Virginia in her glory — contributed to the forces of the frontiersmen. Texas, farther to the south, put her stamp indelibly upon the entire cattle industry of the West. Visionary, impractical, restless, adventurous, these later Elizabethan heroes — bowing to no yoke, insisting on their own rights and scorning often the laws of others, yet careful to retain the best and most advantageous customs of any conquered country — naturally came from those nearest Elizabethan countries which lay abandoned behind them.

If the atmosphere of the Elizabethan Age still

may be found in the forgotten Cumberlands, let us lay claim to kinship with yonder roystering heroes of a gallant day; for this was ever the atmosphere of our own frontier.   To feel again the following breezes of the *Golden Hind*, or see again, floating high in the cloudless skies, the sails of the Great Armada, was the privilege of Americans for a double decade within the memory of men yet living, in that country, so unfailingly beloved, which we call the Old West of America.

CHAPTER II

THE RANGE

WHEN, in 1803, those two immortal youths, Meriwether Lewis and William Clark, were about to go forth on their great journey across the continent, they were admonished by Thomas Jefferson that they would in all likelihood encounter in their travels, living and stalking about, the mammoth or the mastodon, whose bones had been found in the great salt-licks of Kentucky. We smile now at such a supposition; yet it was not unreasonable then. No man knew that tremendous country that lay beyond the mouth of the Missouri.

The explorers crossed one portion of a vast land which was like to nothing they had ever seen — the region later to become the great cattle-range of America. It reached, although they could know nothing of that, from the Spanish possessions on the south across a thousand miles of short-grass lands to the present Canadian boundary line — which certain obdurate American souls still say ought to have been at 54° 40′, and not where it is! From the Rio Grande to "Fifty-four forty," indeed, would have made nice measurements for the Saxon cattle-range.

Little, however, was the value of this land understood by the explorers; and, for more than half a century afterwards, it commonly was supposed to be useless for the occupation of white men and suitable only as a hunting-ground for savage tribes. Most of us can remember the school maps of our own youth, showing a vast region marked, vaguely, "The Great American Desert," which was considered hopeless for any human industry, but much of which has since proved as rich as any land anywhere on the globe.

Perhaps it was the treeless nature of the vast Plains which carried the first idea of their infertility. When the first settlers of Illinois and Indiana came up from south of the Ohio River they had their choice of timber and prairie lands. Thinking the prairies worthless — since land which could not raise a tree certainly could not raise crops—these first occupants of the Middle West spent a generation or more, axe in hand, along the heavily timbered river-bottoms. The prairies were long in settling. No one then could have predicted that farm lands in that region would be worth three hundred dollars an acre or better, and that these prairies of the Mississippi Valley would, in a few generations, be studded with great towns and would form a part of the granary of the world.

But, if our early explorers, passing beyond the valley of the Missouri, found valueless the region of the Plains and the foothills, not so the wild creatures or the savage men who had lived there longer than science records. The buffalo then ranged from the Rio Grande to the Athabaska, from the Missouri to the Rockies, and beyond. No one seems to have concluded in those days that there was after all slight difference between the buffalo and the domestic ox. The native cattle, however, in untold thousands and millions, had even then proved beyond peradventure the sustaining and strengthening nature of the grasses of the Plains.

Now, each creature, even of human species, must adjust itself to its environment. Having done so, commonly it is disposed to love that environment. The Eskimo and the Zulu each thinks that he has the best land in the world. So with the American Indian, who, supported by the vast herds of buffalo, ranged all over that tremendous country which was later to be given over to the white man with his domestic cattle. No freer life ever was lived by any savages than by the Horse Indians of the Plains in the buffalo days; and never has the world known a physically higher type of savage.

On the buffalo-range — that is to say, on the cattle-range which was to be — Lewis and Clark met several bands of the Sioux — the Mandans and the Assiniboines, the Blackfeet, the Shoshones. Farther south were the Pawnees, the Kaws, the Otoes, the Osages, most of whom depended in part upon the buffalo for their living, though the Otoes, the Pawnees, the Mandans, and certain others now and then raised a little corn or a few squashes to help out their bill of fare. Still farther south dwelt the Kiowas, the Comanches, and others. The Arapahoes, the Cheyennes, the Crows, and the Utes, all hunters, were soon to come into the ken of the white man. Of such of these tribes as they met, the youthful captains made accounting, gravely and with extraordinary accuracy, but without discovering in this region much future for Americans. They were explorers and not industrial investigators.

It was nearly half a century after the journey of Lewis and Clark that the Forty-Niners were crossing the Plains, whither, meanwhile, the Mormons had trekked in search of a country where they might live as they liked. Still the wealth of the Plains remained untouched. California was in the eyes of the world. The great cow-range was overleaped. But, in the early fifties, when the placer fields of California began to be less numerous and less rich, the half-savage population of the mines roared on northward, even across our northern line. Soon it was to roll back. Next it worked east and southeast and northeast over the great dry plains of Washington and Oregon, so that, as readily may be seen, the cow-range proper was not settled as most of the West was, by a directly westbound thrust of an eastern population; but, on the contrary, it was approached from several different angles — from the north, from the east, from the west and northwest, and finally from the south.

The early, turbulent population of miners and adventurers was crude, lawless, and aggressive. It cared nothing whatever for the Indian tribes.

War, instant and merciless, where it meant murder for the most part, was set on foot as soon as white touched red in that far western region.

All these new white men who had crowded into the unknown country of the Plains, the Rockies, the Sierras, and the Cascades, had to be fed. They could not employ and remain content with the means by which the red man there had always fed himself. Hence a new industry sprang up in the United States, which of itself made certain history in that land. The business of freighting supplies to the West, whether by bull-train or by pack-train, was an industry *sui generis*, very highly specialized, and pursued by men of great business ability as well as by men of great hardihood and daring.

Each of these freight trains which went West carried hanging on its flank more and more of the white men. As the trains returned, more and more was learned in the States of the new country which lay between the Missouri and the Rockies, which ran no man knew how far north, and no man could guess how far south. Now appears in history Fort Benton, on the Missouri, the great northern supply post — just as at an earlier date there had appeared Fort Hall, one of the old fur-trading posts beyond the Rockies, Bent's Fort on the Arkansas, and many other outposts of the new Saxon civilization in the West.

Later came the pony express and the stage coach which made history and romance for a generation. Feverishly, boisterously, a strong, rugged, woman-less population crowded westward and formed the wavering, now advancing, now receding line of the great frontier of American story.

But for long there was no sign of permanent settlement on the Plains, and no one thought of this region as the frontier. The men there who were prospecting and exploiting were classified as no more than adventurers. No one seems to have taken a lesson from the Indian and the buffalo. The reports of Frémont long since had called attention to the nourishing quality of those grasses of the high country, but the day of the cowboy had not yet dawned. There is a some-what feeble story which runs to the effect that in 1866 one of the great wagon-trains, caught by the early snows of winter, was obliged to abandon its oxen on the range. It was supposed that, of course, the oxen must perish during the winter. But next spring the owners were surprised to find that the oxen, so far from perishing, had flourished very much — indeed, were fat and in good condition. So runs the story which is often repeated. It may be true, but to accredit to this incident the beginnings of the cattle industry in the Indian country would surely be going too far. The truth is that the cow industry was not a Saxon discovery. It was a Latin enterprise, flourishing in Mexico long before the first of these miners and adventurers came on the range.

Something was known of the Spanish lands to the south through the explorations of Pike, but more through the commerce of the prairies — the old wagon trade from the Missouri River to the Spanish cities of Sante Fé and Chihuahua. Now the cow business, south of the Rio Grande, was already well differentiated and developed at the time the first adventurers from the United States went into Texas and began to crowd their Latin neighbors for more room. There it was that our Saxon frontiersmen first discovered the cattle industry. But these southern and northern riflemen — ruthless and savage, yet strangely statesmanlike — though they might betimes drive away the owners of the herds, troubled little about the herds themselves. There was a certain fascination to these rude strangers in the slow and easeful civilization of Old Spain which they encountered in the land below them. Little by little, and then largely and yet more largely, the warriors of San Jacinto reached out and began to claim lands for themselves — leagues and uncounted leagues of land, which had, however, no market value. Well within the memory of the present generation large tracts of good land were bought in Texas for six cents an acre; some was bought for half that price in a time not much earlier. Today much of that land is producing wealth; but land then was worthless — and so were cows.

This civilization of the Southwest, of the new Republic of Texas, may be regarded as the first enduring American result of contact with the Spanish industry. The men who won Texas came mostly from Kentucky and Tennessee or southern Ohio, and the first colonizer of Texas was a Virginian, Stephen Fuller Austin. They came along the old Natchez Trace from Nashville to the Mississippi River — that highway which has so much history of its own. Down this old winding trail into the greatest valley of all the world, and beyond that valley out into the Spanish country, moved steadily the adventurers whose fathers had but recently crossed the Appalachians. One of the strongest thrusts of the American civilization thus entered the cattle-range at its lower end, between the Rio Grande and the Red River.

In all the several activities, mining, freighting, scouting, soldiering, riding pony express, or even sheer adventuring for what might come, there was ever a trading back and forth between home-staying men and adventuring men. Thus there was an interchange of knowledge and of customs between East and West, between our old country and our new. There was an interchange, too, at the south, where our Saxon civilization came in touch with that of Mexico.

We have now to note some fundamental facts and principles of the cattle industry which our American cattlemen took over ready-made from the hands of Mexico.

The Mexicans in Texas had an abundance of small, hardy horses of African and Spanish breed, which Spain had brought into the New World — the same horses that the Moors had brought into Spain — a breed naturally hardy and able to subsist upon dry food. Without such horses there

could have been no cattle industry. These
horses, running wild in herds, had crossed to the
upper Plains. La Vérendrye, and later Lewis
and Clark, had found the Indians using horses
in the north. The Indians, as we have seen, had
learned to manage the horse. Formerly they had
used dogs to drag the *travois*, but now they used
the "elk-dog," as they first called the horse.

In the original cow country, that is, in Mexico
and Texas, countless herds of cattle were held in
a loose sort of ownership over wide and unknown
plains. Like all wild animals in that warm
country, they bred in extraordinary numbers.
The southern range, indeed, has always been
called the breeding range. The cattle had little
value. He who wanted beef killed beef. He who
wanted leather killed cattle for their hides. But
beyond these scant and infrequent uses cattle
had no definite value.

The Mexican, however, knew how to handle
cows. He could ride a horse, and he could rope
cattle and brand them. Most of the cattle of a
wide range would go to certain water-holes more
or less regularly, where they might be roughly
collected or estimated. This coming of the cattle
to the watering-places made it unnecessary for

owners of cattle to acquire ranch land. It was
enough to secure the water-front where the cows
must go to drink. That gave the owner all the
title he needed. His right to the increase he could
prove by another phenomenon of nature, just as
inevitable and invariable as that of thirst. The
maternal instinct of a cow and the dependence of
the calf upon its mother gave the old rancher of
immemorial times sufficient proof of ownership
in the increase of his herd. The calf would run
with its own mother and with no other cow through
its first season. So that if an old Mexican *ranchero*
saw a certain number of cows at his watering-
places, and with them calves, he knew that all
before him were his property — or, at least, he
claimed them as such and used them.

Still, this was loose-footed property. It might
stray away after all, or it might be driven away.
Hence, in some forgotten time, our shrewd Spaniard invented a system of proof of ownership
which has always lain at the very bottom of the
organized cow industry; he invented the method
of branding. This meant his sign, his name, his
trade-mark, his proof of ownership. The animal
could not shake it off. It would not burn off in
the sun or wash off in the rain. It went with the

animal and could not be eradicated from the animal's hide. Wherever the bearer was seen, the brand upon its hide provided certain identification of the owner.

Now, all these basic ideas of the cow industry were old on the lower range in Texas when our white men first drifted thither. The cattle industry, although in its infancy, and although supposed to have no great future, was developed long before Texas became a republic. It never, indeed, changed very much from that time until the end of its own career.

One great principle was accepted religiously even in those early and crude days. A man's cow was *his* cow. A man's brand was *his* brand. There must be no interference with his ownership. Hence certain other phases of the industry followed inevitably. These cattle, these calves, each branded by the iron of the owner, in spite of all precautions, began to mingle as settlers became more numerous; hence came the idea of the round-up. The country was warm and lazy. If a hundred or a thousand cows were not collected, very well. If a calf were separated from its mother, very well. The old ranchers never quarreled among themselves. They never would have made in the

South anything like a cattle association; it was left for the Yankees to do that at a time when cows had come to have far greater values.   There were few arguments in the first *rodeos* of the lower range.   One rancher would vie with his neighbor in generosity in the matter of unbranded calves. Haggling would have been held contemptible.   On the lower range in the old times no one cared much about a cow.   Why should one do so?   There was no market for cows — no one who wished to buy them.   If one tendered a Mexican *cinquo pesos* for a yearling or a two-year-old, the owner might perhaps offer the animal as a gift, or he might smile and say "*Con mucha gusto*" as he was handed a few pieces of silver.   There were plenty of cows everywhere in the world!

Let us, therefore, give the old Spaniard full credit alike in picturesque romance and in the organized industry of the cow.   The westbound thrust which came upon the upper part of the range in the days of more shrewd and exacting business methods was simply the best-known and most published phase of frontier life in the cow country; hence we have usually accepted it as typical.   It would not be accurate to say that the cattle industry was basically much influenced or governed by northern or eastern men. In practically all of its great phenomena the frontier of the old cow-range was southern by birth and growth.

There lay, then, so long unused, that vast and splendid land so soon to write romantic history of its own, so soon to come into the admiration or the wonder of a great portion of the earth — a land of fascinating interest to the youth of every country, and a region whose story holds a charm for young and old alike even today. It was a region royal in its dimensions. Far on the west it was hedged by the gray-sided and white-topped mountains, the Rockies. Where the buffalo once lived, the cattle were to live, high up in the foothills of this great mountain range which ran from the Rio Grande to Canada. On the east, where lay the Prairies rather than the Plains, it was a country waving with high native grasses, with many brilliant flowers hiding among them, the sweet-william, the wild rose, and often great masses of the yellow sunflower.

From the Rio Grande to the Athabaska, for the greater part, the frontier sky was blue and cloudless during most of the year. The rainfall was not great. The atmosphere was dry. It was a cheerful country, one of optimism and not of gloom. In the extreme south, along the Rio Grande, the climate was moister, warmer, more enervating; but on the high steppes of the middle range in Colorado, Wyoming, Montana, western Nebraska, there lay the finest out-of-doors country, man's country the finest of the earth.

But for the time, busy with more accustomed things, mining and freighting and fighting and hunting and trading and trapping, we Americans who had arrived upon the range cared little for cows. The upper thrust of the great herds from the south into the north had not begun. It was after the Civil War that the first great drives of cattle from the south toward the north began, and after men had learned in the State of Texas that cattle moved from the Rio Grande to the upper portions of the State and fed on the mesquite grass would attain greater stature than in the hot coast country. Then swiftly, somewhat luridly, there leaped into our comprehension and our interest that strange country long loosely held under our flag, the region of the Plains, the region which we now call the Old West.

In great bands, in long lines, slowly, low-headed, sore-footed, the vast gatherings of the prolific lower range moved north, each cow with its title indelibly marked upon its hide. These cattle were now going to take the place of those on which the Indians had depended for their living these many years. A new day in American history had dawned.

CHAPTER III

THE CATTLE TRAILS

THE customary method of studying history by means of a series of events and dates is not the method which we have chosen to employ in this study of the Old West. Speaking generally, our minds are unable to assimilate a condensed mass of events and dates; and that is precisely what would be required of us if we should attempt here to follow the ways of conventional history. Dates are at best no more than milestones on the pathway of time; and in the present instance it is not the milestones but the road itself with which we are concerned. Where does the road begin? Why comes it hither? Whither does it lead? These are the real questions.

Under all the exuberance of the life of the range there lay a steady business of tremendous size and enormous values. The "uproarious iniquity" of the West, its picturesqueness, its vividness —

these were but froth on the stream. The stream itself was a steady and somber flood. Beyond this picturesqueness of environment very few have cared to go, and therefore sometimes have had little realization of the vastness of the cowboy's kingdom, the "magnitude of the interests in his care, or the fortitude, resolution, and instant readiness essential to his daily life." The American cowboy is the most modern representative of a human industry that is second to very few in antiquity.

Virgil strikes the note of real history: *Quorum pars magna fui*, says Æneas — "Of which I was a great part." If we seek the actual truth, we ought most to value contemporary records, representations made by men who were themselves a part of the scenes which they describe. In that way we shall arrive not merely upon lurid events, not alone upon the stereotyped characters of the "Wild West," but upon causes which are much more interesting and immensely more valuable than any merely titillating stories from the weirdly illustrated Apocrypha of the West. We must go below such things if we would gain a just and lasting estimate of the times. We ought to look on the old range neither as a playground

of idle men nor as a scene of hysterical and
contorted human activities. We ought to look
upon it from the point of view of its uses to
mankind. The explorers found it a wilderness,
the home of the red man and the buffalo. What
were the underlying causes of its settlement and
development?

There is in history no agency so wondrous in
events, no working instrumentality so great as
transportation. The great seeking of all human
life is to find its level. Perhaps the first men
traveled by hollowed logs down stream. Then
possibly the idea of a sail was conceived. Early
in the story of the United States men made commercial journeys from the head of the Ohio to the
mouth of the Mississippi by flatboats, and came
back by keelboats. The pole, the cordelle, the
paddle, and the sail, in turn helped them to navi-
gate the great streams which led out into the
West. And presently there was to come that tremendous upheaval wrought by the advent of the
iron trails which, scorning alike waterways and
mountain ranges, flung themselves almost directly
westward across the continent.

The iron trails, crossing the northern range soon
after the Civil War, brought a market to the cattle

country. Inevitably the men of the lower range would seek to reach the railroads with what they had to sell — their greatest natural product, cattle on the hoof. This was the primary cause of the great northbound drives already mentioned, the greatest pastoral phenomena in the story of the world.

The southern herds at that time had no market at their doors. They had to go to the market, and they had to go on foot. That meant that they must be driven northward by cattle handlers who had passed their days in the wild life of the lower range. These cowmen of course took their character and their customs northward with them, and so they were discovered by those enthusiastic observers, newly arrived by rail, whom the cowmen were wont to call "pilgrims."

Now the trail of the great cattle drives — the Long Trail — was a thing of tremendous importance of itself and it is still full of interest. As it may not easily be possible for the author to better a description of it that was written some twenty years ago, that description is here again set down.[1]

[1] *The Story of the Cowboy,* by E. Hough. Appleton. 1897. Reprinted by permission.

The braiding of a hundred minor pathways, the Long Trail lay like a vast rope connecting the cattle country of the South with that of the North. Lying loose or coiling, it ran for more than two thousand miles along the eastern edge of the Rocky Mountains, sometimes close in at their feet, again hundreds of miles away across the hard tablelands or the well-flowered prairies. It traversed in a fair line the vast land of Texas, curled over the Indian Nations, over Kansas, Colorado, Nebraska, Wyoming, and Montana, and bent in wide overlapping circles as far west as Utah and Nevada; as far east as Missouri, Iowa, even Illinois; and as far north as the British possessions. Even today you may trace plainly its former course, from its faint beginnings in the lazy land of Mexico, the Ararat of the cattle-range. It is distinct across Texas, and multifold still in the Indian lands. Its many intermingling paths still scar the iron surface of the Neutral Strip, and the plows have not buried all the old furrows in the plains of Kansas. Parts of the path still remain visible in the mountain lands of the far North. You may see the ribbons banding the hillsides today along the valley of the Stillwater, and along the Yellow-

stone and toward the source of the Missouri.
The hoof marks are beyond the Musselshell,
over the Bad Lands and the coulees and the
flat prairies; and far up into the land of the
long cold you may see, even today if you like,
the shadow of that unparalleled pathway, the
Long Trail of the cattle-range. History has no
other like it.

The Long Trail was surveyed and constructed in
a century and a day. Over the Red River of the
South, a stream even today perhaps known but
vaguely in the minds of many inhabitants of the
country, there appeared, almost without warning,
vast processions of strange horned kine — processions of enormous wealth, owned by kings who
paid no tribute, and guarded by men who never
knew a master. Whither these were bound, what
had conjured them forth, whence they came, were
questions in the minds of the majority of the
population of the North and East to whom the
phenomenon appeared as the product of a day.
The answer to these questions lay deep in the laws
of civilization, and extended far back into that
civilization's history. The Long Trail was finished in a day. It was begun more than a century before that day, and came forward along the

very appointed ways of time. . . . Thus, far
down in the vague Southwest, at some distant
time, in some distant portion of old, mysterious
Mexico, there fell into line the hoof prints which
made the first faint beginnings of the Long Trail,
merely the path of a half nomadic movement
along the line of the least resistance.

The Long Trail began to deepen and extend.
It received then, as it did later, a baptism of human
blood such as no other pathway of the continent
has known. The nomadic and the warlike days
passed, and there ensued a more quiet and pastoral time. It was the beginning of a feudalism
of the range, a barony rude enough, but a glorious
one, albeit it began, like all feudalism, in large-
handed theft and generous murdering. The flocks
of these strong men, carelessly interlapping, increased and multiplied amazingly. They were
hardly looked upon as wealth. The people could
not eat a tithe of the beef; they could not use a
hundredth of the leather. Over hundreds and
hundreds of miles of ownerless grass lands, by
the rapid waters of the mountains, by the slow
streams of the plains or the long and dark lagoons
of the low coast country, the herds of tens grew
into droves of hundreds and thousands and hun-

dreds of thousands. This was really the dawning
of the American cattle industry.

Chips and flakes of the great Southwestern herd
began to be seen in the Northern States. As early
as 1857 Texas cattle were driven to Illinois. In
1861 Louisiana was, without success, tried as an
outlet. In 1867 a venturous drover took a herd
across the Indian Nations, bound for California,
and only abandoned the project because the Plains
Indians were then very bad in the country to the
north. In 1869 several herds were driven from
Texas to Nevada. These were side trails of the
main cattle road. It seemed clear that a great
population in the North needed the cheap beef of
Texas, and the main question appeared to be
one of transportation. No proper means for this
offered. The Civil War stopped almost all plans
to market the range cattle, and the close of that
war found the vast grazing lands of Texas covered
fairly with millions of cattle which had no actual
or determinate value. They were sorted and
branded and herded after a fashion, but neither
they nor their increase could be converted into
anything but more cattle. The cry for a market
became imperative.

Meantime the Anglo-Saxon civilization was rolling swiftly toward the upper West. The Indians were being driven from the Plains. A solid army was pressing behind the vanguard of soldier, scout, and plainsman. The railroads were pushing out into a new and untracked empire. They carried the market with them. The market halted, much nearer, though still some hundred of miles to the north of the great herd. The Long Trail tapped no more at the door of Illinois, Missouri, Arkansas, but leaped north again definitely, this time springing across the Red River and up to the railroads, along sharp and well-defined channels deepened in the year of 1866 alone by the hoofs of more than a quarter of a million cattle.

In 1871, only five years later, over six hundred thousand cattle crossed the Red River for the Northern markets. Abilene, Newton, Wichita, Ellsworth, Great Bend, Dodge, flared out into a swift and sometime evil blossoming. Thus the men of the North first came to hear of the Long Trail and the men who made it, although really it had begun long ago and had been foreordained to grow.

By this time, 1867 and 1868, the northern portions of the region immediately to the east of the

Rocky Mountains had been sufficiently cleared of their wild inhabitants to admit a gradual though precarious settlement. It had been learned yet again that the buffalo grass and the sweet waters of the far North would fatten a range broadhorn to a stature far beyond any it could attain on the southern range. The Long Trail pushed rapidly even farther to the north where there still remained "free grass" and a new market. The territorial ranges needed many thousands of cattle for their stocking, and this demand took a large part of the Texas drive which came to Abilene, Great Bend, and Fort Dodge. Moreover, the Government was now feeding thousands of its new red wards, and these Indians needed thousands of beeves for rations, which were driven from the southern range to the upper army posts and reservations. Between this Government demand and that of the territorial stock ranges there was occupation for the men who made the saddle their home.

The Long Trail, which had previously found the black corn lands of Illinois and Missouri, now crowded to the West, until it had reached Utah and Nevada, and penetrated every open park and mesa and valley of Colorado, and found all the high plains of Wyoming. Cheyenne and Laramie became common words now, and drovers spoke as wisely of the dangers of the Platte as a year before they had mentioned those of the Red River or the Arkansas. Nor did the Trail pause in its irresistible push to the north until it had found the last of the five great transcontinental lines, far in the British provinces. Here in spite of a long season of ice and snow the uttermost edges of the great herd might survive, in a certain percentage at least, each year in an almost unassisted struggle for existence, under conditions different enough, it would seem, from those obtaining at the opposite extreme of the wild roadway over which they came.

The Long Trail of the cattle-range was done! By magic the cattle industry had spread over the entire West. Today many men think of that industry as belonging only to the Southwest, and many would consider that it was transferred to the North. Really it was not transferred but extended, and the trail of the old drive marks the line of that extension.

Today the Long Trail is replaced by other trails, product of the swift development of the West, and it remains as the connection, now for the most part historical only, between two phases of an industry which, in spite of differences of climate and condition, retain a similarity in all essential features. When the last steer of the first herd was driven into the corral at the Ultima Thule of the range, it was the pony of the American cowboy which squatted and wheeled under the spur and burst down the straggling street of the little frontier town. Before that time, and since that time, it was and has been the same pony and the same man who have traveled the range, guarding and guiding the wild herds, from the romantic to the commonplace days of the West.

CHAPTER IV

THE COWBOY

THE Great West, vast and rude, brought forth men also vast and rude. We pass today over parts of that matchless region, and we see the red hills and ragged mountain-fronts cut and crushed into huge indefinite shapes, to which even a small imagination may give a human or more than human form. It would almost seem that the same great hand which chiseled out these monumental forms had also laid its fingers upon the people of this region and fashioned them rude and ironlike, in harmony with the stern faces set about them.

Of all the babes of that primeval mother, the West, the cowboy was perhaps her dearest because he was her last. Some of her children lived for centuries; this one for not a triple decade before he began to be old. What was really the life of this child of the wild region of America, and what were the conditions of the experience that bore him, can never be fully known by those who have not seen the West with wide eyes — for the cowboy was simply a part of the West. He who does not understand the one can never understand the other.

If we care truly to see the cowboy as he was and seek to give our wish the dignity of a real purpose, we should study him in connection with his surroundings and in relation to his work. Then we shall see him not as a curiosity but as a product— not as an eccentric driver of horned cattle but as a man suited to his times.

Large tracts of that domain where once the cowboy reigned supreme have been turned into farms by the irrigator's ditch or by the dry-farmer's plan. The farmer in overalls is in many instances his own stockman today. On the ranges of Arizona, Wyoming, and Texas and parts of Nevada we may find the cowboy, it is true, even today: but he is no longer the Homeric figure that once dominated the plains. In what we say as to his trade, therefore, or his fashion in the practice of it, we speak in terms of thirty or forty years ago, when wire was unknown, when the round-up still was necessary, and the cowboy's life was indeed that of the open.

By the costume we may often know the man.
The cowboy's costume was harmonious with its
surroundings.   It was planned upon lines of such
stern utility as to leave no possible thing which we
may call dispensable.   The typical cowboy costume could hardly be said to contain a coat and
waistcoat.   The heavy woolen shirt, loose and
open at the neck, was the common wear at all
seasons of the year excepting winter, and one has
often seen cowboys in the winter-time engaged in
work about the yard or corral of the ranch wearing no other cover for the upper part of the body
but one or more of these heavy shirts.   If the
cowboy wore a coat he would wear it open and
loose as much as possible.   If he wore a "vest"
he would wear it slouchily, hanging open or
partly unbuttoned most of the time.   There was
a reason for this slouchy habit.   The cowboy
would say that the vest closely buttoned about
the body would cause perspiration, so that the
wearer would quickly chill upon ceasing exercise.
If the wind were blowing keenly when the cowboy dismounted to sit upon the ground for din-
ner, he would button up his waistcoat and be
warm.   If it were very cold he would button up
his coat also.

The cowboy's boots were of fine leather and fitted tightly, with light narrow soles, extremely small and high heels. Surely a more irrational foot-covering never was invented; yet these tight, peaked cowboy boots had a great significance and may indeed be called the insignia of a calling. There was no prouder soul on earth than the cowboy. He was proud of being a horseman and had a contempt for all human beings who walked. On foot in his tight-toed boots he was lost; but he wished it to be understood that he never was on foot. If we rode beside him and watched his seat in the big cow saddle we found that his high and narrow heels prevented the slipping forward of the foot in the stirrup, into which he jammed his feet nearly full length. If there was a fall, the cowboy's foot never hung in the stirrup. In the corral roping, afoot, his heels anchored him. So he found his little boots not so unserviceable and retained them as a matter of pride. Boots made for the cowboy trade sometimes had fancy tops of bright-colored leather. The Lone Star of Texas was not infrequent in their ornamentation.

The curious pride of the horseman extended also to his gloves. The cowboy was very careful in the selection of his gloves. They were made of the

finest buckskin, which could not be injured by
wetting.   Generally they were tanned white and
cut with a deep cuff or gauntlet from which hung
a little fringe to flutter in the wind when he rode
at full speed on horseback.

The cowboy's hat was one of the typical and
striking features of his costumes. It was a heavy,
wide, white felt hat with a heavy leather band
buckled about it.   There has been no other head
covering devised so suitable as the Stetson for the
uses of the Plains, although high and heavy black
hats have in part supplanted it today among
stockmen. The boardlike felt was practically
indestructible.   The brim flapped a little and, in
time, was turned up and perhaps held fast to the
crown by a thong.   The wearer might sometimes
stiffen the brim by passing a thong through a
series of holes pierced through the outer edge.   He
could depend upon his hat in all weathers.   In
the rain it was an umbrella; in the sun a shield;
in the winter he could tie it down about his ears
with his handkerchief.

Loosely thrown about the cowboy's shirt collar
was a silk kerchief.   It was tied in a hard knot
in front, and though it could scarcely be said to
be devoted to the uses of a neck scarf, yet it was

a great comfort to the back of the neck when one was riding in a hot wind. It was sure to be of some bright color, usually red. Modern would-be cow-punchers do not willingly let this old kerchief die, and right often they over-play it. For the cowboy of the "movies," however, let us register an unqualified contempt. The real range would never have been safe for him.

A peculiar and distinctive feature of the cowboy's costume was his "chaps" (*chaparéjos*). The chaps were two very wide and full-length trouser-legs made of heavy calfskin and connected by a narrow belt or strap. They were cut away entirely at front and back so that they covered only the thigh and lower legs and did not heat the body as a complete leather garment would. They were intended solely as a protection against branches, thorns, briers, and the like, but they were prized in cold or wet weather. Sometimes there was seen, more often on the southern range, a cowboy wearing chaps made of skins tanned with the hair on; for the cowboy of the Southwest early learned that goatskin left with the hair on would turn the cactus thorns better than any other material. Later, the chaps became a sort of affectation on the part of new men on the range; but the old-time cowboy wore them for use, not as a uniform. In hot weather he laid them off.

In the times when some men needed guns and all men carried them, no pistol of less than 44-caliber was tolerated on the range, the solid framed 45-caliber being the one almost universally used. The barrel was eight inches long, and it shot a rifle cartridge of forty grains of powder and a blunt-ended bullet that made a terrible missile. This weapon depended from a belt worn loose resting upon the left hip and hanging low down on the right hip so that none of the weight came upon the abdomen. This was typical, for the cowboy was neither fancy gunman nor army officer. The latter carries the revolver on the left, the butt pointing forward.

An essential part of the cow-puncher's outfit was his "rope." This was carried in a close coil at the side of the saddle-horn, fastened by one of the many thongs scattered over the saddle. In the Spanish country it was called *reata* and even today is sometimes seen in the Southwest made of rawhide. In the South it was called a *lariat*. The modern rope is a well-made three-quarter-inch hemp rope about thirty feet in length, with a leather or rawhide eye. The cowboy's quirt was a short heavy whip, the stock being of wood or iron covered with braided leather and carrying a lash made of two or three heavy loose thongs. The spur in the old days had a very large rowel with blunt teeth an inch long. It was often ornamented with little bells or oblongs of metal, the tinkling of which appealed to the childlike nature of the Plains rider. Their use was to lock the rowel.

His bridle — for, since the cowboy and his mount are inseparable, we may as well speak of his horse's dress also — was noticeable for its tremendously heavy and cruel curbed bit, known as the "Spanish bit." But in the ordinary riding and even in the exciting work of the old round-up and in "cutting out," the cowboy used the bit very little, nor exerted any pressure on the reins. He laid the reins against the neck of the pony opposite to the direction in which he wished it to go, merely turning his hand in the direction and inclining his body in the same way. He rode with the pressure of the knee and the inclination of the body and the light side-shifting of both reins. The saddle was the most important part of the outfit. It was a curious thing, this saddle developed by the cattle trade, and the world has

no other like it. Its great weight — from thirty
to forty pounds — was readily excusable when one
remembers that it was not only seat but work-
bench for the cowman. A light saddle would be
torn to pieces at the first rush of a maddened
steer, but the sturdy frame of a cow-saddle would
throw the heaviest bull on the range. The high
cantle would give a firmness to the cowboy's seat
when he snubbed a steer with a sternness sufficient to send it rolling heels over head. The
high pommel, or "horn," steel-forged and covered
with cross braids of leather, served as anchor
post for this same steer, a turn of the rope
about it accomplishing that purpose at once.
The saddle-tree forked low down over the pony's
back so that the saddle sat firmly and could not
readily be pulled off. The great broad cinches
bound the saddle fast till horse and saddle were
practically one fabric. The strong wooden house
of the old heavy stirrup protected the foot from
being crushed by the impact of the herd. The
form of the cow-saddle has changed but little, although today one sees a shorter seat and smaller
horn, a "swell front" or roll, and a stirrup of open
"ox-bow" pattern.

The round-up was the harvest of the range.

The time of the calf round-up was in the spring after the grass had become good and after the calves had grown large enough for the branding. The State Cattle Association divided the entire State range into a number of round-up districts. Under an elected round-up captain were all the bosses in charge of the different ranch outfits sent by men having cattle in the round-up. Let us briefly draw a picture of this scene as it was.

Each cowboy would have eight or ten horses for his own use, for he had now before him the hardest riding of the year. When the cow-puncher went into the herd to cut out calves he mounted a fresh horse, and every few hours he again changed horses, for there was no horse which could long endure the fatigue of the rapid and intense work of cutting. Before the rider stretched a sea of interwoven horns, waving and whirling as the densely packed ranks of cattle closed in or swayed apart. It was no prospect for a weakling, but into it went the cow-puncher on his determined little horse, heeding not the plunging, crushing, and thrusting of the excited cattle. Down under the bulks of the herd, half hid in the whirl of dust, he would spy a little curly calf running, dodging, and twisting, always at the heels of its mother; and he would dart

4

in after, following the two through the thick of surging and plunging beasts. The sharp-eyed pony would see almost as soon as his rider which cow was wanted and he needed small guidance from that time on. He would follow hard at her heels, edging her constantly toward the flank of the herd, at times nipping her hide as a reminder of his own superiority. In spite of herself the cow would gradually turn out toward the edge, and at last would be swept clear of the crush, the calf following close behind her. There was a whirl of the rope and the calf was laid by the heels and dragged to the fire where the branding irons were heated and ready.

Meanwhile other cow-punchers are rushing calves to the branding. The hubbub and turmoil increase. Taut ropes cross the ground in many directions. The cutting ponies pant and sweat, rear and plunge. The garb of the cowboy is now one of white alkali which hangs gray in his eyebrows and moustache. Steers bellow as they surge to and fro. Cows charge on their persecutors. Fleet yearlings break and run for the open, pursued by men who care not how or where they ride.

We have spoken in terms of the past. There is

no calf round-up of the open range today. The last of the round-ups was held in Routt County, Colorado, several years ago, so far as the writer knows, and it had only to do with shifting cattle from the summer to the winter range.

'After the calf round-up came the beef round-up, the cowman's final harvest. This began in July or August. Only the mature or fatted animals were cut out from the herd. This "beef cut" was held apart and driven on ahead from place to place as the round-up progressed. It was then driven in by easy stages to the shipping point on the railroad, whence the long trainloads of cattle went to the great markets.

In the heyday of the cowboy it was natural that his chief amusements should be those of the outdoor air and those more or less in line with his employment. He was accustomed to the sight of big game, and so had the edge of his appetite for its pursuit worn off. Yet he was a hunter, just as every Western man was a hunter in the times of the Western game. His weapons were the rifle, revolver, and rope; the latter two were always with him. With the rope at times he captured the coyote, and under special conditions he has taken deer and even antelope in this way, though this

was of course most unusual and only possible under chance conditions of ground and cover.   Elk
have been roped by cowboys many times, and
it is known that even the mountain sheep has been
so taken, almost incredible as that may seem.
The young buffalo were easy prey for the cowboy
and these he often roped and made captive.   In
fact the beginnings of all the herds of buffalo now
in captivity in this country were the calves roped
and secured by cowboys; and these few scattered
individuals of a grand race of animals remain as
melancholy reminders alike of a national shiftless-
ness and an individual skill and daring.

The grizzly was at times seen by the cowboys
on the range, and if it chanced that several cowboys were together it was not unusual to give him
chase.   They did not always rope him, for it was
rarely that the nature of the country made this
possible.   Sometimes they roped him and wished
they could let him go, for a grizzly bear is uncom-
monly active and straightforward in his habits
at close quarters.   The extreme difficulty of such
a combat, however, gave it its chief fascination for
the cowboy.   Of course, no one horse could hold
the bear after it was roped, but, as one after another came up, the bear was caught by neck and

foot and body, until at last he was tangled and tripped and haled about till he was helpless, strangled, and nearly dead. It is said that cowboys have so brought into camp a grizzly bear, forcing him to half walk and half slide at the end of the ropes. No feat better than this could show the courage of the plainsman and of the horse which he so perfectly controlled.

Of such wild and dangerous exploits were the cowboy's amusements on the range. It may be imagined what were his amusements when he visited the "settlements." The cow-punchers, reared in the free life of the open air, under circumstances of the utmost freedom of individual action, perhaps came off the drive or round-up after weeks or months of unusual restraint or hardship, and felt that the time had arrived for them to "celebrate." Merely great rude children, as wild and untamed and untaught as the herds they led, they regarded their first look at the "settlements" of the railroads as a glimpse of a wider world. They pursued to the uttermost such avenues of new experience as lay before them, almost without exception avenues of vice. It is strange that the records of those days should be chosen by the public to be held as the measure of the American cowboy. Those days were brief, and they are long since gone. The American cowboy atoned for them by a quarter of a century of faithful labor.

The amusements of the cowboy were like the features of his daily surroundings and occupation — they were intense, large, Homeric. Yet, judged at his work, no higher type of employee ever existed, nor one more dependable. He was the soul of honor in all the ways of his calling. The very blue of the sky, bending evenly over all men alike, seemed to symbolize his instinct for justice. Faithfulness and manliness were his chief traits; his standard — to be a "square man."

Not all the open range will ever be farmed, but very much that was long thought to be irreclaimable has gone under irrigation or is being more or less successfully "dry-farmed." The man who brought water upon the arid lands of the West changed the entire complexion of a vast country and with it the industries of that country. Acres redeemed from the desert and added to the realm of the American farmer were taken from the realm of the American cowboy.

The West has changed. The curtain has

dropped between us and its wild and stirring scenes. The old days are gone. The house dog sits on the hill where yesterday the coyote sang. There are fenced fields and in them stand sleek round beasts, deep in crops such as their ancestors never saw. In a little town nearby is the hurry and bustle of modern life. This town is far out upon what was called the frontier, long after the frontier has really gone. Guarding its ghost here stood a little army post, once one of the pillars, now one of the monuments of the West.

Out from the tiny settlement in the dusk of evening, always facing toward where the sun is sinking, might be seen riding, not so long ago, a figure we should know. He would thread the little lane among the fences, following the guidance of hands other than his own, a thing he would once have scorned to do. He would ride as lightly and as easily as ever, sitting erect and jaunty in the saddle, his reins held high and loose in the hand whose fingers turn up gracefully, his whole body free yet firm in the saddle with the seat of the perfect horseman. At the boom of the cannon, when the flag dropped fluttering down to sleep, he would rise in his stirrups and wave his hat to the flag. Then, toward the edge, out into the evening, he would ride on. The dust of his riding would mingle with the dusk of night. We could not see which was the one or the other. We could only hear the hoof-beats passing, boldly and steadily still, but growing fainter, fainter, and more faint. [1]

[1] For permission to use in this chapter material from the author's *The Story of the Cowboy*, acknowledgment is made to D. Appleton & Co.

CHAPTER V

THE MINES

IF the influence of the cattle industry was paramount in the development of the frontier region found by the first railways, it should not be concluded that this upthrust of the southern cattle constituted the only contribution to the West of that day. There were indeed earlier influences, the chief of which was the advent of the wild population of the placer mines. The riches of the gold-fields hastened the building of the first transcontinental railroads and the men of the mines set their mark also indelibly upon the range.

It is no part of our business here to follow the great discoveries of 1849 in California.[1] Neither shall we chronicle the once-famous rushes from California north into the Fraser River Valley of British Columbia; neither is it necessary to mention in much detail the great camps of Nevada;

[1] See Stewart Edward White: *The Forty-Niners* (*Chronicles of America*).

nor yet the short-lived stampede of 1859 to the
Pike's Peak country in Colorado.   The rich placer
fields of Idaho and Montana, from which enormous amounts were taken, offer typical examples
of the mining communities of the Rockies.

We may never know how much history remains
forever unwritten.   Of the beginnings of the
Idaho camps there have trickled back into record
only brief, inconsequent, and partial stories.   The
miners who surged this way and that all through
the Sierras, the upper Cascades, north into the
Selkirks, and thence back again into the Rockies
were a turbulent mob.   Having overrun all our
mountain ranges, following the earlier trails of
the traders and trappers, they now recoiled upon
themselves and rolled back eastward to meet the
advancing civilization of the westbound rails, car-
ing nothing for history and less for the civilized
society in which they formerly had lived.   This
story of bedlam broken loose, of men gone crazed
by the sudden subversion of all known values and
all standards of life, was at first something which
had no historian and can be recorded only by
way of hearsay stories which do not always tally
as to the truth.

The mad treasure-hunters of the California

mines, restless, insubordinate, incapable of restraint, possessed of the belief that there might
be gold elsewhere than in California, and having
heard reports of strikes to the north, went hurrying out into the mountains of Oregon and Washington, in a wild stampede, all eager again to
engage in the glorious gamble where by one
lucky stroke of the pick a man might be set
free of the old limitations of human existence.

So the flood of gold-seekers — passing north into
the Fraser River country, south again into Oregon
and Washington, and across the great desert plains
into Nevada and Idaho — made new centers of
lurid activity, such as Oro Fino, Florence, and
Carson. Then it was that Walla Walla and Lewiston, outfitting points on the western side of the
range, found place upon the maps of the land,
such as they were.

Before these adventurers, now eastbound and
no longer facing west, there arose the vast and
formidable mountain ranges which in their time
had daunted even the calm minds of Meriwether
Lewis and William Clark. But the prospectors
and the pack-trains alike penetrated the Salmon
River Range. Oro Fino, in Idaho, was old in
1861. The next great strikes were to be made

around Florence. Here the indomitable packer from the West, conquering unheard-of difficulties, brought in whiskey, women, pianos, food, mining-tools. Naturally all these commanded fabulous prices. The price for each and all lay underfoot. Man, grown superman, could overleap time itself by a stroke of the pick! What wonder delirium reigned!

These events became known in the Mississippi Valley and farther eastward. And now there came hurrying out from the older regions many more hundreds and thousands eager to reach a land not so far as California, but reputed to be quite as rich. It was then, as the bull-trains came in from the East, from the head of navigation on the Missouri River, that the western outfitting points of Walla Walla and Lewiston lost their importance.

Southward of the Idaho camps the same sort of story was repeating itself. Nevada had drawn to herself a portion of the wild men of the stampedes. Carson for its day (1859–60) was a capital not unlike the others. Some of its men had come down from the upper fields, some had arrived from the East over the old Santa Fé Trail, and yet others had drifted in from California.

All the camps were very much alike. A straggling row of log cabins or huts of motley construction; a few stores so-called, sometimes of logs, or, if a saw-mill was at hand, of rude sawn boards; a number of saloons, each of which customarily also supported a dance-hall; a series of cabins or huts where dwelt individual men, each doing his own cooking and washing; and outside these huts the uptorn earth — such were the camps which dotted the trails of the stampedes across inhospitable deserts and mountain ranges. Church and school were unknown. Law there was none, for of organized society there was none. The women who lived there were unworthy of the name of woman. The men strode about in the loose dress of the camp, sometimes without waistcoat, sometimes coatless, shod with heavy boots, always armed.

If we look for causes contributory to the history of the mining-camp, we shall find one which ordinarily is overlooked — the invention of Colt's revolving pistol. At the time of the Civil War, though this weapon was not old, yet it had attained very general use throughout the frontier. That was before the day of modern ammunition. The six-shooter of the placer days was of the old cap-and-ball type, heavy, long-barreled, and usually wooden-handled. It was the general ownership of these deadly weapons which caused so much bloodshed in the camps. The revolver in the hands of a tyro is not especially serviceable, but it attained great deadliness in the hands of an expert user. Such a man, naturally of quick nerve reflexes, skillful and accurate in the use of the weapon through long practice, became a dangerous, and for a time an unconquerable, antagonist.

It is a curious fact that the great Montana fields were doubly discovered, in part by men coming east from California, and in part by men passing west in search of new gold-fields. The first discovery of gold in Montana was made on Gold Creek by a half-breed trapper named François, better known as Be-net-see. This was in 1852, but the news seems to have lain dormant for a time — naturally enough, for there was small ingress or egress for that wild and unknown country. In 1857, however, a party of miners who had wandered down the Big Hole River on their way back east from California decided to look into the Gold Creek discovery, of which they had heard. This party was led by James and Granville Stuart, and among others in the

party were Jake Meeks, Robert Hereford, Robert
Dempsey, John W. Powell, John M. Jacobs,
Thomas Adams, and some others. These men
did some work on Gold Creek in 1858, but seem
not to have struck it very rich, and to have
withdrawn to Fort Bridger in Utah until the
autumn of 1860. Then a prospector by the name
of Tom Golddigger turned up at Bridger with
additional stories of creeks to the north, so that
there was a gradual straggling back toward Gold
Creek and other gulches. This prospector had
been all over the Alder Gulch, which was ere
long to prove fabulously rich.

It was not, however, until 1863 that the Montana camps sprang into fame. It was not Gold
Creek or Alder Gulch, but Florence and other
Idaho camps, that, in the summer and autumn of
1862, brought into the mountains no less than five
parties of gold-seekers, who remained in Montana
because they could not penetrate the mountain
barrier which lay between them and the Salmon
River camps in Idaho.

The first of these parties arrived at Gold Creek
by wagon-train from Fort Benton and the second
hailed from Salt Lake. An election was held for
the purpose of forming a sort of community or-

ganization, the first election ever known in Montana. The men from the East had brought with them some idea of law and organization. There were now in the Montana fields many good men such as the Stuart Brothers, Samuel T. Hauser, Walter Dance, and others later well known in the State. These men were prominent in the organization of the first miners' court, which had occasion to try — and promptly to hang — Stillman and Jernigan, two ruffians who had been in from the Salmon River mines only about four days when they thus met retribution for their early crimes. An associate of theirs, Arnett, had been killed while resisting arrest. The reputation of Florence for lawlessness and bloodshed was well known; and, as the outrages of the well-organized band of desperadoes operating in Idaho might be expected to begin at any time in Montana, a certain uneasiness existed among the newcomers from the States.

Two more parties, likewise bound for Idaho and likewise baffled by the Salmon River range, arrived at the Montana camps in the same summer. Both these were from the Pike's Peak country in Colorado. And in the autumn came a fifth — this one under military protection, Captain James L. Fisk commanding, and having in the party a number of settlers bound for Oregon as well as miners for Idaho. This expedition arrived in the Prickly Pear Valley in Montana on September 21, 1862, having left St. Paul on the 16th of June, traveling by steamboat and wagon-train. While Captain Fisk and his expedition pushed on to Walla Walla, nearly half of the immigrants stayed to try their luck at placer-mining. But the yield was not great and the distant Salmon River mines, their original destination, still awaited them. Winter was approaching. It was now too late in the season to reach the Salmon River mines, five hundred miles across the mountains, and it was four hundred miles to Salt Lake, the nearest supply post; therefore, most of the men joined this little army of prospectors in Montana. Some of them drifted to the Grasshopper diggings, soon to be known under the name of Bannack — one of the wildest mining-camps of its day.

These different origins of the population of the first Montana camps are interesting because of the fact that they indicate a difference in the two currents of population which now met here in the new placer fields. In general the wildest and most desperate of the old-time adventurers, those coming from the West, had located in the Idaho camps, and might be expected in Montana at any time. In contrast to these, the men lately out from the States were of a different type, many of them sober, most of them law-abiding, men who had come out to better their fortunes and not merely to drop into the wild and licentious life of a placer-camp. Law and order always did prevail eventually in any mining community. In the case of Montana, law and order arrived almost synchronously with lawlessness and desperadoism.

Law and order had not long to wait before the arrival of the notorious Henry Plummer and his band from Florence. Plummer was already known as a bad man, but was not yet recognized as the leader of that secret association of robbers and murderers which had terrorized the Idaho camps. He celebrated his arrival in Bannack by killing a man named Cleveland. He was acquitted in the miners' court that tried him, on the usual plea of self-defense. He was a man of considerable personal address.

The same tribunal soon assembled once more to try three other murderers, Moore, Reeves, and Mitchell, with the agreement that the men should have a jury and should be provided with counsel.

They were all practically freed; and after that the roughs grew bolder than ever. The Plummer band swore to kill every man who had served in that court, whether as juryman or officer. So well did they make good their threat that out of the twenty-seven men thus engaged all but seven were either killed or driven out of the country, nine being murdered outright. The man who had acted as sheriff of this miners' court, Hank Crawford, was unceasingly hounded by Plummer, who sought time and again to fix a quarrel on him. Plummer was the best shot in the mountains at that time, and he thought it would be easy for him to kill his man and enter the usual plea of self-defense. By good fortune, however, Crawford caught Plummer off his guard and fired upon him with a rifle, breaking his right arm. Plummer's friends called in Dr. Glick, the best physician in Bannack, to treat the wounded man, warning him that if he told anything about the visit he would be shot down. Glick held his peace, and later was obliged to attend many of the wounded outlaws, who were always engaged in affairs with firearms.

Of all these wild affrays, of the savage life which they denoted, and of the stern ways in which retribution overtook the desperadoes of the mines, there is no better historian than Nathaniel P. Langford, a prominent citizen of the West, who accompanied the overland expedition of 1862 and took part in the earliest life of Montana. His work, *Vigilante Days and Ways*, is an invaluable contemporary record.

It is mentally difficult for us now fully to restore these scenes, although the events occurred no earlier than the Civil War. "Life in Bannack at this time," says Langford, "was perfect isolation from the rest of the world. Napoleon was not more of an exile on St. Helena than a newly arrived immigrant from the States in this region of lakes and mountains. All the great battles of the season of 1862 — Antietam, Fredericksburg, Second Bull Run — all the exciting debates of Congress, and the more exciting combats at sea, first became known to us on the arrival of newspapers and letters in the spring of 1863."

The Territory of Idaho, which included Montana and nearly all Wyoming, was organized March 3, 1863. Previous to that time western Montana and Idaho formed a part of Washington Territory, of which Olympia was the capital, and Montana, east of the mountains, belonged to the Territory of Dakota, of which the capital was Yankton, on the Missouri. Langford makes clear the political uncertainties of the time, the difficulty of enforcing the laws, and narrates the circumstances which led to the erection in 1864 of the new Territory of Montana, comprising the limits of the present State.[1]

In Montana as elsewhere in these days of great sectional bitterness, there was much political strife; and this no doubt accounts for an astonishing political event that now took place. Henry Plummer, the most active outlaw of his day, was elected sheriff and entrusted with the enforcement of the laws! He made indeed a great show of enforcing the laws. He married, settled down, and for a time was thought by some of the ill-

[1] The Acts of Congress organizing Territories and admitting States are milestones in the occupation of this last West. On the eve of the Civil War, Kansas was admitted into the Union; during the war, the Territories of Colorado, Nevada, Dakota, Arizona, Idaho, and Montana were organized, and Nevada was admitted as a State. Immediately after the war, Nebraska was admitted and Wyoming was organized as a Territory. In the Centennial Year (1876) Colorado became a State. In 1889 and 1890 North and South Dakota, Montana, Washington, Idaho, and Wyoming were admitted as States. In the latter year Oklahoma was carved out of the Indian Territory. Utah with its Mormon population was kept waiting at the doors of the Union until 1896. Oklahoma became a State in 1907; Arizona and New Mexico were admitted in 1912.

advised to have reformed his ways, although in truth he could not have reformed.

By June, 1863, the extraordinarily rich strike in Alder Gulch had been made.   The news of this spread like wildfire to Bannack and to the Salmon River mines in Idaho as well, and the result was one of the fiercest of all the stampedes, and the rise, almost overnight, of Virginia City.   Meanwhile some Indian fighting had taken place and in a pitched battle on the Bear River General Connor had beaten decisively the Bannack Indians, who for years had preyed on the emigrant trains. This made travel on the mountain trails safer than it had been; and the rich Last Chance Gulch on which the city of Helena now stands attracted a tremendous population almost at once.   The historian above cited lived there.   Let him tell of the life.

One long stream of active life filled the little creek on its auriferous course from Bald Mountain, through a canyon of wild and picturesque character, until it emerged into the large and fertile valley of the Pas-sam-a-ri . . . the mountain stream called by Lewis and Clark in their journal "Philanthropy River."   Lateral streams of great beauty pour down the sides of the mountain chain bounding the valley. . . . Gold placers were found upon these streams and occupied soon after the settlement at Virginia City was commenced. . . . This human hive, numbering at least ten thousand people, was the product of ninety days. Into it were crowded all the elements of a rough and active civilization. Thousands of cabins and tents and brush wakiups . . . were seen on every hand. Every foot of the gulch . . . was undergoing displacement, and it was already disfigured by huge heaps of gravel which had been passed through the sluices and rifled of their glittering contents. . . . Gold was abundant, and every possible device was employed by the gamblers, the traders, the vile men and women that had come in with the miners into the locality, to obtain it. Nearly every third cabin was a saloon where vile whiskey was peddled out for fifty cents a drink in gold dust. Many of these places were filled with gambling tables and gamblers. . . . Hurdy-gurdy dance-houses were numerous. . . . Not a day or night passed which did not yield its full fruition of vice, quarrels, wounds, or murders. The crack of the revolver was often heard above the merry notes of the violin. Street fights were frequent, and as no one knew when or where they would occur, every one was on his guard against a random shot.

Sunday was always a gala day. . . . The stores were all open. . . . Thousands of people crowded the thoroughfares ready to rush in the direction of any promised excitement. Horse-racing was among the most favored amusements. Prize rings were formed, and brawny men engaged in fisticuffs until their sight was lost and their bodies pommelled to a jelly, while hundreds of onlookers cheered the victor. . . . Pistols flashed, bowie knives flourished, and braggart oaths filled the air, as often as men's passions triumphed over their reason. This was indeed the reign of unbridled license, and men who at first regarded it with disgust and terror, by constant exposure soon learned to become a part of it and forget that they had ever been aught else. All classes of society were represented at this general exhibition. Judges, lawyers, doctors, even clergymen, could not claim exemption. Culture and religion afforded feeble protection, where allurement and indulgence ruled the hour.

Imagine, therefore, a fabulously rich mountain valley twelve miles in extent, occupied by more than ten thousand men and producing more than ten millions of dollars before the close of the first year! It is a stupendous demand on any imagination. How might all this gold be sent out in safe-keeping? We are told that the only stage route extended from Virginia City no farther than Bannack. Between Virginia City and Salt Lake City there was an absolute wilderness, wholly unsettled, four hundred and seventy-five miles in width. "There was no post office in the Territory. Letters were brought from Salt Lake first at a cost of two dollars and a half each, and later in the season at one dollar each. All money at infinite risk was sent to the nearest express office at Salt Lake City by private hands."

Practically every man in the new gold-fields was aware of the existence of a secret band of well-organized ruffians and robbers. The general feeling was one of extreme uneasiness. There were plenty of men who had taken out of the ground considerable quantities of gold, and who would have been glad to get back to the East with their little fortunes, but they dared not start. Time after time the express coach, the solitary rider, the unguarded wagon-train, were held up and robbed, usually with the concomitant of murder. When the miners did start out from one camp to another they took all manner of precautions to conceal their gold dust. We are told that on one occasion one party bored a hole in the end of the wagon tongue with an auger and filled it full of gold dust, thus escaping observation! The robbers learned to know the express agents, and always had advice of every large shipment of gold. It was almost useless to undertake to conceal anything from them; and resistance was met with death. Such a reign of terror, such an organized system of highway robbery, such a light valuing of human life, has been seldom found in any other time or place.

There were, as we have seen, good men in these

camps — although the best of them probably let
down the standards of living somewhat after their
arrival there; but the trouble was that the good
men did not know one another, had no organization, and scarcely dared at first to attempt one.
On the other hand, the robbers' organization was
complete and kept its secrets as the grave;
indeed, many and many a lonesome grave held
secrets none ever was to know.   How many men
went out from Eastern States and disappeared,
their fate always to remain a mystery, is a part
of the untold story of the mining frontier.

There are known to have been a hundred and
two men killed by Plummer and his gang; how
many were murdered without their fate ever being
discovered can not be told.   Plummer was the
leader of the band, but, arch-hypocrite that he
was, he managed to keep his own connection with
it a secret.   His position as sheriff gave him many
advantages.   He posed as being a silver-mine
expert, among other things, and often would be
called out to "expert" some new mine.   That
usually meant that he left town in order to com-
mit some desperate robbery.   The boldest outrages always required Plummer as the leader.
Sometimes he would go away on the pretense of

following some fugitive from justice. His horse, the fleetest in the country, often was found, laboring and sweating, at the rear of his house. That meant that Plummer had been away on some secret errand of his own. He was suspected many times, but nothing could be fastened upon him; or there lacked sufficient boldness and sufficient organization on the part of the law-and-order men to undertake his punishment.

We are not concerned with repeating thrilling tales, bloody almost beyond belief, and indicative of an incomprehensible depravity in human nature, so much as we are with the causes and effects of this wild civilization which raged here quite alone in the midst of one of the wildest of the western mountain regions. It will best serve our purpose to retain in mind the twofold character of this population, and to remember that the frontier caught to itself not only ruffians and desperadoes, men undaunted by any risk, but also men possessed of a yet steadier personal courage and hardihood. There were men rough, coarse, brutal, murderous; but against them were other men self-reliant, stern, just, and resolved upon fair play.

That was indeed the touchstone of the entire

civilization which followed upon the heels of these scenes of violence. It was fair play which really animated the great Montana Vigilante movement and which eventually cleaned up the merciless gang of Henry Plummer and his associates. The centers of civilization were far removed. The courts were powerless. In some cases even the machinery of the law was in the hands of these ruffians. But so violent were their deeds, so brutal, so murderous, so unfair, that slowly the indignation of the good men arose to the white-hot point of open resentment and of swift retribution. What the good men of the frontier loved most of all was justice. They now enforced justice in the only way left open to them. They did this as California earlier had done; and they did it so well that there was small need to repeat the lesson.

The actual extermination of the Henry Plummer band occurred rather promptly when the Vigilantes once got under way. One of the band by the name of Red Yager, in company with yet another by the name of Brown, had been concerned in the murder of Lloyd Magruder, a merchant of the Territory. The capture of these two followed closely upon the hanging of George Ives, also accused of more than one murder. Ives was an example of the degrading influence of the mines. He was a decent young man until he left his home in Wisconsin. He was in California from 1857 to 1858. When he appeared in Idaho he seemed to have thrown off all restraint and to have become a common rowdy and desperado. It is said of him that "few men of his age ever had been guilty of so many fiendish crimes."

Yager and Brown, knowing the fate which Ives had met, gave up hope when they fell into the hands of the newly organized Vigilantes. Brown was hanged; so was Yager; but Yager, before his death, made a full confession which put the Vigilantes in possession of information they had never yet been able to secure.[1]

Much has been written and much romanced

---

[1] Langford gives these names disclosed by Yager as follows: "Henry Plummer was chief of the band; Bill Bunton, stool pigeon and second in command; George Brown, secretary; Sam Bunton, roadster; Cyrus Skinner, fence, spy, and roadster; George Shears, horse thief and roadster; Frank Parish, horse thief and roadster; Hayes Lyons, telegraph man and roadster; Bill Hunter, telegraph man and roadster; Ned Ray, council-room keeper at Bannack City; George Ives, Stephen Marshland, Dutch John (Wagner), Alex Carter, Whiskey Bill (Graves), Johnny Cooper, Buck Stinson, Mexican Frank, Bob Zachary, Boone Helm, Clubfoot George (Lane), Billy Terwiliger, Gad Moore, were roadsters." Practically all these were executed by the Vigilantes, with many others, and eventually the band of outlaws was entirely broken up.

about the conduct of these desperadoes when
they met their fate. Some of them were brave
and some proved cowards at the last. For a
time, Plummer begged abjectly, his eyes stream-
ing with tears. Suddenly he was smitten with
remorse as the whole picture of his past life
appeared before him. He promised everything,
begged everything, if only life might be spared
him — asked his captors to cut off his ears, to cut
out his tongue, then strip him naked and banish
him. At the very last, however, he seems to
have become composed. Stinson and Ray went
to their fate alternately swearing and whining.
Some of the ruffians faced death boldly. More
than one himself jumped from the ladder or
kicked from under him the box which was the
only foothold between him and eternity. Boone
Helm was as hardened as any of them. This
man was a cannibal and murderer. He seems
to have had no better nature whatever. His
last words as he sprang off were "Hurrah for
Jeff Davis! Let her rip!" Another man re-
marked calmly that he cared no more for hanging than for drinking a glass of water. But each
after his own fashion met the end foreordained
for him by his own lack of compassion; and of

compassion he received none at the hands of the men who had resolved that the law should be established and should remain forever.

There was an instant improvement in the social life of Virginia City, Bannack, and the adjoining camps as soon as it was understood that the Vigilantes were afoot. Langford, who undoubtedly knew intimately of the activities of this organization, makes no apology for the acts of the Vigilantes, although they did not have back of them the color of the actual law. He says:

The retribution dispensed to these daring freebooters in no respect exceeded the demands of absolute justice. . . . There was no other remedy. Practically the citizens had no law, but if law had existed it could not have afforded adequate redress. This was proven by the feeling of security consequent upon the destruction of the band. When the robbers were dead the people felt safe, not for themselves alone but for their pursuits and their property. They could travel without fear. They had reasonable assurance of safety in the transmission of money to the States and in the arrival of property over the unguarded route from Salt Lake. The crack of pistols had ceased, and they could walk the streets without constant exposure to danger. There was an omnipresent spirit of protection, akin to that omnipresent spirit of law which pervaded older and more civilized communities. . . . Young men who had learned to believe that the roughs were destined to rule and who, under the influence of that faith, were fast drifting into crime shrunk appalled before the thorough work of the Vigilantes. Fear, more potent than conscience, forced even the worst of men to observe the requirements of society, and a feeling of comparative security among all classes was the result.

Naturally it was not the case that all the bad men were thus exterminated. From time to time there appeared vividly in the midst of these surroundings additional figures of solitary desperadoes, each to have his list of victims, and each himself to fall before the weapons of his enemies or to meet the justice of the law or the sterner meed of the Vigilantes. It would not be wholly pleasant to read even the names of a long list of these; perhaps it will be sufficient to select one, the notorious Joseph Slade, one of the "picturesque" characters of whom a great deal of inaccurate and puerile history has been written. The truth about Slade is that he was a good man at first, faithful in the discharge of his duties as an agent of the stage company. Needing at times to use violence lawfully, he then began to use it unlawfully. He drank and soon went from bad to worse. At length his outrages became so numerous that the men of the community took him out and hanged him. His fate taught many others the risk of going too far in defiance of law and decency.

What has been true regarding the camps of Florence, Bannack, and Virginia City, had been true in part in earlier camps and was to be repeated perhaps a trifle less vividly in other camps yet to come. The Black Hills gold rush, for instance, which came after the railroad but before the Indians were entirely cleared away, made a certain wild history of its own. We had our Deadwood stage line then, and our Deadwood City with all its wild life of drinking, gambling, and shooting — the place where more than one notorious bad man lost his life, and some capable officers of the peace shared their fate. To describe in detail the life of this stampede and the wild scenes ensuing upon it is perhaps not needful here. The main thing is that the great quartz lodes of the Black Hills support in the end a steady, thrifty, and law-abiding population.

All over that West, once so unspeakably wild and reckless, there now rise great cities where recently were scattered only mining-camps scarce fit to be called units of any social compact. It was but yesterday that these men fought and

6

drank and dug their own graves in their own sluices. At the city of Helena, on the site of Last Chance Gulch, one recalls that not so long ago citizens could show with a certain contemporary pride the old dead tree once known as "Hangman's Tree." It marked a spot which might be called a focus of the old frontier. Around it, and in the country immediately adjoining, was fought out the great battle whose issue could not be doubted — that between the new and the old days; between law and order and individual lawlessness; between the school and the saloon; between the home and the dance-hall; between society united and resolved and the individual reverted to worse than savagery.

CHAPTER VI

THE PATHWAYS OF THE WEST

Since we have declared ourselves to be less interested in bald chronology than in the naturally connected causes of events which make chronology worth while, we may now, perhaps, double back upon the path of chronology, and take up the great early highways of the West — what we might call the points of attack against the frontier.

The story of the Santa Fé Trail, now passing into oblivion, once was on the tongue of every man. This old highroad in its heyday presented the most romantic and appealing features of the earlier frontier life. The Santa Fé Trail was the great path of commerce between our frontier and the Spanish towns trading through Santa Fé. This commerce began in 1822, when about threescore men shipped certain goods across the lower Plains by pack-animals. By 1826 it was employing a hundred men and was using wagons and mules. In 1830, when oxen first were used on the trail, the trade amounted to $120,000 annually; and by 1843, when the Spanish ports were closed, it had reached the value of $450,000, involving the use of 230 wagons and 350 men. It was this great wagon trail which first brought us into touch with the Spanish civilization of the Southwest. Its commercial totals do not bulk large today, but the old trail itself was a thing titanic in its historic value.

This was the day not of water but of land transport; yet the wheeled vehicles which passed out into the West as common carriers of civilization clung to the river valleys — natural highways and natural resting places of home-building man. This has been the story of the advance of civilization from the first movements of the world's peoples. The valleys are the cleats of civilization's golden sluices.

There lay the great valley of the Arkansas, offering food and water, an easy grade and a direct course reaching out into the West, even to the edge of the lands of Spain; and here stood wheeled vehicles able to traverse it and to carry dry-goods and hardware, and especially domestic cotton fabrics, which formed the great staple of

a "Santa Fé assortment." The people of the
Middle West were now, in short, able to feed and
clothe themselves and to offer a little of their
surplus merchandise to some one else in sale.
They had begun to export! Out yonder, in a
strange and unknown land, lay one of the original markets of America!

On the heels of Lewis and Clark, who had just
explored the Missouri River route to the Northwest, Captain Zebulon Pike of the Army, long
before the first wheeled traffic started West, had
employed this valley of the Arkansas in his search
for the southwestern delimitations of the United
States. Pike thought he had found the head of
the Red River when after a toilsome and dangerous march he reached the headwaters of the Rio
Grande. But it was not our river. It belonged
to Spain, as he learned to his sorrow, when he
marched all the way to Chihuahua in old Mexico
and lay there during certain weary months.

It was Pike's story of the far Southwest that
first started the idea of the commerce of the
Santa Fé Trail. In that day geography was a
human thing, a thing of vital importance to all
men. Men did not read the stock markets; they
read stories of adventure, tales of men returned

from lands out yonder in the West. Heretofore
the swarthy Mexicans, folk of the dry plains and
hills around the head of the Rio Grande and the
Red, had carried their cotton goods and many
other small and needful things all the way from
Vera Cruz on the seacoast, over trails that were
long, tedious, uncertain, and expensive. A far
shorter and more natural trade route went west
along the Arkansas, which would bring the American goods to the doors of the Spanish settlements.
After Pike and one or two others had returned
with reports of the country, the possibilities of
this trade were clear to any one with the merchant's imagination.

There is rivalry for the title of "Father of the
Santa Fé Trail." As early as 1812, when the
United States was at war with England, a party
of men on horseback trading into the West, commonly called the McKnight, Baird, and Chambers party, made their way west to Santa Fé.
There, however, they met with disaster. All their
goods were confiscated and they themselves lay in
Mexican jails for nine years. Eventually the re-
turning survivors of this party told their stories,
and those stories, far from chilling, only inflamed
the ardor of other adventurous traders. In 1821

more than one American trader reached Santa
Fé; and, now that the Spanish yoke had been
thrown off by the Mexicans, the goods, instead
of being confiscated, were purchased eagerly.

It is to be remembered, of course, that trading
of this sort to Mexico was not altogether a new
thing. Sutlers of the old fur traders and trappers
already had found the way to New Spain from
the valley of the Platte, south along the eastern
edge of the Rockies, through Wyoming and
Colorado. By some such route as that at least
one trader, a French creole, agent of the firm
of Bryant & Morrison at Kaskaskia, had penetrated to the Spanish lands as early as 1804, while
Lewis and Clark were still absent in the upper
wilderness. Each year the great mountain ren-
dezvous of the trappers — now at Bent's Fort
on the Arkansas, now at Horse Creek in Wyoming, now on Green River in Utah, or even farther beyond the mountains — demanded supplies
of food and traps and ammunition to enable the
hunters to continue their work for another year.
Perhaps many of the pack-trains which regularly
supplied this shifting mountain market already
had traded in the Spanish country.

It is not necessary to go into further details

regarding this primitive commerce of the prairies. It yielded a certain profit; it shaped the character of the men who carried it on. But what is yet more important, it greatly influenced the country which lay back of the border on the Missouri River. It called yet more men from the eastern settlements to those portions which lay upon the edge of the Great Plains. There crowded yet more thickly, up to the line between the certain and the uncertain, the restless westbound population of all the country.

If on the south the valley of the Arkansas led outward to New Spain, yet other pathways made out from the Mississippi River into the unknown lands. The Missouri was the first and last of our great natural frontier roads. Its lower course swept along the eastern edge of the Plains, far to the south, down to the very doors of the most adventurous settlements in the Mississippi Valley. Those who dared its stained and turbulent current had to push up, onward, northward, past the mouth of the Platte, far to the north across degrees of latitude, steadily forward through a vast virgin land. Then the river bent boldly and strongly off to the west, across another empire. Its great falls indicated that it headed high; beyond the great falls its steady sweep westward and at last southward, led into yet other kingdoms.

When we travel by horse or by modern motor car in that now accessible region and look about us, we should not fail to reflect on the long trail of the upbound boats which Manuel Lisa and other traders sent out almost immediately upon the return of the Lewis and Clark expedition. We should see them struggling up against that tremendous current before steam was known, driven by their lust for new lands. We may then understand fully what we have read of the enterprises of the old American Fur Company, and bring to mind the forgotten names of Campbell and Sublette, of General Ashley and of Wyeth — names to be followed by others really of less importance, as those of Bonneville and Frémont. That there could be farms, that there ever might be homes, in this strange wild country, was, to these early adventurers, unthinkable.

Then we should picture the millions of buffalo which once covered these plains and think of the waste and folly of their slaughtering. We should see the long streams of the Mackinaw boats swimming down the Missouri, bound for St. Louis, laden with bales of buffalo and beaver peltry, every pound of which would be worth ten dollars at the capital of the fur trade; and we should restore to our minds the old pictures of savage tribesmen, decked in fur-trimmed war-shirts and plumed bonnets, armed with lance and sinewed bow and bull-neck shield, not forgetting whence they got their horses and how they got their food.

The great early mid-continental highway, known as the Oregon Trail or the Overland Trail, was by way of the Missouri up the Platte Valley, thence across the mountains. We know more of this route because it was not discontinued, but came steadily more and more into use, for one reason after another. The fur traders used it, the Forty-Niners used it, the cattlemen used it in part, the railroads used it; and, lastly, the settlers and farmers used it most of all.

In physical features the Platte River route was similar to that of the Arkansas Valley. Each at its eastern extremity, for a few days' travel, passed over the rolling grass-covered and flower-besprinkled prairies ere it broke into the high and dry lands of the Plains, with their green or grey or brown covering of practically flowerless short grasses. But between the two trails of the Arkansas and the Platte there existed certain wide differences. At the middle of the nineteenth century the two trails were quite distinct in personnel, if that word may be used. The Santa Fé Trail showed Spanish influences; that of the Platte Valley remained far more nearly American.

Thus far the frontier had always been altering the man who came to it; and, indirectly, always altering those who dwelt back of the frontier, nearer to the Appalachians or the Atlantic. A new people now was in process of formation — a people born of a new environment. America and the American were conceiving. There was soon to be born, soon swiftly to grow, a new and lasting type of man. Man changes an environment only by bringing into it new or better transportation. Environment changes man. Here in the mid-continent, at the mid-century, the frontier and the ways of the frontier were writing their imprint on the human product of our land.

The first great caravans of the Platte Valley, when the wagon-trains went out hundreds strong, were not the same as the scattering cavalcade of the fur hunters, not the same as the ox-trains and mule-trains of the Santa Fé traffic. The men who wore deepest the wheel marks of the Oregon Trail were neither trading nor trapping men, but home-building men — the first real emigrants to go West with the intent of making homes beyond the Rockies.

The Oregon Trail had been laid out by the explorers of the fur trade. Zealous missionaries had made their way over the trail in the thirties. The Argonauts of '49 passed over it and left it only after crossing the Rockies. But, before gold in California was dreamed of, there had come back to the States reports of lands rich in resources other than gold, lying in the far Northwest, beyond the great mountain ranges; and, before the Forty-Niners were heard of, farmers, home-builders, emigrants, men with their families, men with their household goods, were steadily passing out for the far-off and unknown country of Oregon.

The Oregon Trail was the pathway for Frémont in 1842, perhaps the most overvalued explorer of all the West; albeit this comment may to some seem harsh. Kit Carson and Bill Williams led Frémont across the Rockies almost by the hand. Carson and Williams themselves had been taken across by the Indian tribes. But Frémont could write; and the story which he set down of his first expedition inflamed the zeal of all. Men began to head out for that far-away country beyond the Rockies. Not a few scattered bands, but very many, passed up the valley of the Platte. There began a tremendous trek of thousands of men who wanted homes somewhere out beyond the frontier. And that was more than ten years before the Civil War. The cow trade was not dreamed of; the coming cow country was overleaped and ignored.

Our national horizon extended immeasurably along that dusty way. In the use of the Oregon Trail we first began to be great. The chief figure of the American West, the figure of the ages, is not the long-haired, fringed-legging man riding a raw-boned pony, but the gaunt and sad-faced woman sitting on the front seat of the wagon, following her lord where he might lead, her face hidden in the same ragged sunbonnet which had crossed the Appalachians and the Missouri long before. That was America, my brethren! There was the seed of America's wealth. There was the great romance of all America — the woman in the sunbonnet; and not, after all, the hero with the rifle across his saddle horn. Who has written her story? Who has painted her picture?

They were large days, those of the great Oregon Trail, not always pleasingly dramatic, but oftentimes tragic and terrible. We speak of the Oregon Trail, but it means little to us today; nor will any mere generalities ever make it mean much to us. But what did it mean to the men and women of that day? What and who were those men and women? What did it mean to take the Overland Trail in the great adventure of abandoning forever the known and the safe and setting out for Oregon or California at a time when everything in the far West was new and unknown? How did those good folk travel? Why and whither did they travel?

There is a book done by C. F. McGlashan, a resident of Truckee, California, known as *The History of the Donner Party*, holding a great deal of actual history. McGlashan, living close to Donner Lake, wrote in 1879, describing scenes with which he was perfectly familiar, and recounting facts which he had from direct association with participants in the ill-fated Donner Party. He chronicles events which happened in 1846 —

a date before the discovery of gold in California. The Donner Party was one of the typical American caravans of homeseekers who started for the Pacific Slope with no other purpose than that of founding homes there, and with no expectation of sudden wealth to be gained in the mines. I desire therefore to quote largely from the pages of this book, believing that, in this fashion, we shall come upon history of a fundamental sort, which shall make us acquainted with the men and women of that day, with the purposes and the ambitions which animated them, and with the hardships which they encountered.

The States along the Mississippi were but sparsely settled in 1846, yet the fame of the fruitfulness, the healthfulness, and the almost tropical beauty of the land bordering the Pacific, tempted the members of the Donner Party to leave their homes. These homes were situated in Illinois, Iowa, Tennessee, Missouri, and Ohio. Families from each of these States joined the train and participated in its terrible fate; yet the party proper was organized in Sangamon County, Illinois, by George and Jacob Donner and James F. Reed. Early in April, 1846, the party set out from Springfield, Illinois, and by the first week in May reached Independence, Missouri. Here the party was increased by additional members, and the train comprised about one hundred persons. . . .

In the party were aged fathers with their trusting families about them, mothers whose very lives were wrapped up in their children, men in the prime and vigor of manhood, maidens in all the sweetness and freshness of budding womanhood, children full of glee and mirthfulness, and babes nestling on maternal breasts. Lovers there were, to whom the journey was tinged with rainbow hues of joy and happiness, and strong, manly hearts whose constant support and encouragement was the memory of dear ones left behind in homeland.

The wonderment which all experience in viewing the scenery along the line of the old emigrant road was peculiarly vivid to these people. Few descriptions had been given of the route, and all was novel and unexpected. In later years the road was broadly and deeply marked, and good camping grounds were distinctly indicated. The bleaching bones of cattle that had perished, or the broken fragments of wagons or castaway articles, were thickly strewn on either side of the highway. But in 1846 the way was through almost trackless valleys waving with grass, along rivers where few paths were visible, save those made by the feet of buffalo and antelope, and over mountains and plains where little more than the westward course of the sun guided the travelers. Trading-posts were stationed at only a few widely distant points, and rarely did the party meet with any human beings, save wandering bands of Indians. Yet these first days are spoken of by all of the survivors as being crowned with peaceful enjoyment and pleasant anticipations. There were beautiful flowers by the roadside, an abundance of game in the meadows and mountains, and at night there were singing, dancing, and innocent plays.   Several musical instruments, and many excellent voices, were in the party, and the kindliest feeling and good-fellowship prevailed among the members.

The formation of the company known as the Donner Party was purely accidental.   The union of so many emigrants into one train was not occasioned by any pre-concerted arrangement.   Many composing the Donner Party were not aware, at the outset, that such a tide of emigration was sweeping to California.   In many instances small parties would hear of the mammoth train just ahead of them or just behind them, and by hastening their pace, or halting for a few days, joined themselves to the party.   Many were with the train during a portion of the journey, but from some cause or other became parted from the Donner company before reaching Donner Lake.   Soon after the train left Independence it contained between two and three hundred wagons, and when in motion was two miles in length.   The members of the party proper numbered ninety.

This caravan, like many others of the great assemblage westbound at that time, had great extremes in personnel.   Some were out for mere adventure; some were single men looking for a location.   Most of them were fathers of families, among them several persons of considerable means and of good standing in the community which they were leaving.   While we may suppose that most of them were folk of no extraordinary sort, certainly some were persons of education and intelligence. Among these was the wife of George Donner — Tamsen Donner, a woman of education, a musician, a linguist, a botanist, and of the most sublime heroism.

Tamsen Donner sent back now and then along the route some story of the daily doings of the caravan; and such letters as these are of the utmost interest to any who desire precise information of that time. It would seem that the emigrants themselves for a great part of their route met with no great adventures, nor indeed, appeared to be undertaking any unusual affair. They followed a route up the Platte Valley already long known to those of the eastern settlements.

NEAR THE JUNCTION OF THE NORTH
AND SOUTH PLATTE, June 16, 1846.

MY OLD FRIEND: We are now on the Platte, two hundred miles from Fort Laramie. Our journey so far has been pleasant, the roads have been good, and food plentiful. The water for part of the way has been indifferent, but at no time have our cattle suffered for it. Wood is now very scarce, but "buffalo chips" are excellent; they kindle quickly and retain heat surprisingly. We had this morning buffalo steaks broiled upon them that had the same flavor they would have had upon hickory coals.

We feel no fear of Indians; our cattle graze quietly around our encampment unmolested. Two or three men will go hunting twenty miles from camp; and last night two of our men lay out in the wilderness rather than ride their horses after a hard chase.

Indeed, if I do not experience something far worse than I have yet done, I shall say the trouble is all in getting started. Our wagons have not needed much repair, and I can not yet tell in what respects they could be improved. Certain it is, they can not be too strong. Our preparations for the journey might have been in some respects bettered.

Bread has been the principal article of food in our camp. We laid in one hundred and fifty pounds of flour and seventy-five pounds of meat for each individual, and I fear bread will be scarce. Meat is abundant. Rice and beans are good articles on the road; cornmeal too, is acceptable. Linsey dresses are the most suitable for children. Indeed, if I had one, it would be acceptable. There is so cool a breeze at all times on the Plains that the sun does not feel so hot as one would suppose.

We are now four hundred and fifty miles from Independence. Our route at first was rough, and through a timbered country, which appeared to be fertile. After striking the prairie, we found a first-rate road, and the only difficulty we have had, has been in crossing the creeks. In that, however, there has been no danger.

I never could have believed we could have traveled so far with so little difficulty. The prairie between the Blue and the Platte Rivers is beautiful beyond description. Never have I seen so varied a country, so suitable for cultivation.   Everything is new and pleasing; the Indians frequently come to see us, and the chiefs of a tribe breakfasted at our tent this morning.   All are so friendly that I can not help feeling sympathy and friendship for them.   But on one sheet what can I say?

Since we have been on the Platte, we have had the river on one side and the ever varying mounds on the other, and have traveled through the bottom lands from one to two miles wide, with little or no timber. The soil is sandy, and last year, on account of the dry season, the emigrants found grass here scarce.   Our cattle are in good order, and when proper care has been taken, none have been lost.   Our milch cows have been of great service, indeed.   They have been of more advantage than our meat.   We have plenty of butter and milk.

We are commanded by Captain Russell, an amiable man.   George Donner is himself yet.   He crows in the morning and shouts out, "Chain up, boys — chain up," with as much authority as though he was "something in particular."   John Denton is still with us. We find him useful in the camp.   Hiram Miller and Noah James are in good health and doing well.   We have of the best people in our company, and some, too, that are not so good.

Buffalo show themselves frequently.   We have found the wild tulip, the primrose, the lupine, the eardrop, the larkspur, and creeping hollyhock, and a beautiful flower resembling the bloom of the beech tree, but in bunches as large as a small sugarloaf, and of every variety of shade, to red and green.

I botanize, and read some, but cook "heaps" more.

There are four hundred and twenty wagons, as far as we have heard, on the road between here and Oregon and California.

Give our love to all inquiring friends. God bless them.

Yours truly,

MRS. GEORGE DONNER.

By the Fourth of July the Donner Party had reached Fort Laramie. They pushed on west over the old trail up the Sweetwater River and across the South Pass, the easiest of all the mountain passes known to the early travelers. Without much adventure they reached Fort Bridger, then only a trading-post. Here occurred the fatal mistake of the Donner Party.

Some one at the fort strongly advised them to take a new route, a cut-off said to shorten the distance by about three hundred miles. This cut-off passed along the south shore of Great Salt Lake and caught up the old California Trail from Fort Hall — then well established and well known — along the Humboldt River. The great Donner caravan delayed for some days at Fort Bridger, hesitating over the decision of which route to follow. The party divided. All those who took the old road north of Salt Lake by way of Fort Hall reached California in complete safety. Of the original Donner Party there remained eighty-seven persons. All of these took the cut-off, being eager to save time in their travel. They reached Salt Lake after unspeakable difficulties. Farther west, in the deserts of Nevada, they lost many of their cattle.

Now began among the party dissensions and grumblings. The story is a long one. It reached its tragic dénouement just below the summit of the Sierras, on the shores of Donner Lake. The words of McGlashan may now best serve our purpose.

Generally, the ascent of the Sierra brought joy and gladness to weary overland emigrants. To the Donner Party it brought terror and dismay. The company had hardly obtained a glimpse of the mountains, ere the winter storm clouds began to assemble their hosts around the loftier crests. Every day the weather appeared more ominous and threatening. The delay at the Truckee Meadows had been brief, but every day ultimately cost a dozen lives. On the twenty-third of October, they became thoroughly alarmed at the angry heralds of the gathering storm, and with all haste resumed the journey. It was too late! At Prosser Creek, three miles below Truckee, they found themselves encompassed with six inches of snow. On the summits, the snow was from two to five feet in depth. This was October 28, 1846. Almost a month earlier than usual, the Sierra had donned its mantle of ice and snow. The party were prisoners!

All was consternation. The wildest confusion prevailed. In their eagerness, many went far in advance of the main train. There was little concert of action or harmony of plan. All did not arrive at Donner Lake the same day. Some wagons and families did not reach the lake until the thirty-first day of October, some never went farther than Prosser Creek, while others, on the evening of the twenty-ninth, struggled through the snow, and reached the foot of the precipitous cliffs between the summit and the upper end of the lake. Here, baffled, wearied, disheartened, they turned back to the foot of the lake.

These emigrants did not lack in health, strength, or resolution, but here they were in surroundings absolutely new to them. A sort of panic seized them now. They scattered; their organization disintegrated. All thought of conjoint action, of a social compact, a community of interests, seems to have left them. It was a history of every man for himself, or at least every family for itself. All track of the road was now lost under the snow. At the last pitch up to the summit of the Sierras precipitous cliffs abounded. No one knew the way. And now the snows came once again.

The emigrants suffered a thousand deaths. The pitiless snow came down in large, steady masses. All

understood that the storm meant death.   One of the
Indians silently wrapped his blanket about him and
in deepest dejection seated himself beside a tall pine.
In this position he passed the entire night, only moving
occasionally to keep from being covered with snow.
Mrs. Reed spread down a shawl, placed her four children — Virginia, Patty, James, and Thomas — thereon,
and putting another shawl over them, sat by the side
of her babies during all the long hours of darkness.
Every little while she was compelled to lift the upper
shawl and shake off the rapidly accumulating snow.

With slight interruptions, the storm continued
several days.   The mules and oxen that had always
hovered about camp were blinded and bewildered by
the storm, and straying away were literally buried alive
in the drifts.   What pen can describe the horror of the
position in which the emigrants found themselves?   It
was impossible to move through the deep, soft snow
without the greatest effort.   The mules were gone, and
were never found.   Most of the cattle had perished,
and were wholly hidden from sight.   The few oxen
which were found were slaughtered for beef.

The travelers knew that the supplies they had
could not last long.   On the 12th of November a
relief party essayed to go forward, but after struggling a short distance toward the summit, came
back wearied and broken-hearted, unable to make
way through the deep, soft snow.   Then some one
— said to have been F. W. Graves of Vermont —
bethought himself of making snowshoes out of

the oxbows and the hides of the slaughtered oxen. With these they did better.

Volunteers were called for yet another party to cross the mountains into California. Fifteen persons volunteered. Not all of them were men —some were mothers, and one was a young woman. Their mental condition was little short of desperation. Only, in the midst of their intense hardships it seemed to all, somewhere to the westward was California, and that there alone lay any hope. The party traveled four miles the first day; and their camp fires were visible below the summit. The next day they traveled six miles and crossed the divide.

They were starving, cold, worn out, their feet frozen to bursting, their blood chilled. At times they were caught in some of the furious storms of the Sierras. They did not know their way. On the 27th of December certain of the party resolved themselves to that last recourse which alone might mean life. Surrounded by horrors as they were, it seemed they could endure the thought of yet an additional horror. . . . There were the dead, the victims who already had perished! . . .

Seven of the fifteen got through to the Sacramento Valley, among these the young girl, Mary Graves, described as "a very beautiful girl, of tall and slender build, and exceptionally graceful character." The story brought out by these survivors of the first party to cross the Sierras from the starving camp set all California aflame. There were no less than three relief expeditions formed, which at varying dates crossed the mountains to the east. Some men crossed the snow belt five times in all. The rescuers were often in as much danger as the victims they sought to save.

And they could not save them. Back there in their tents and hovels around Donner Lake starvation was doing its work steadily. There is contemporary history also covering the details of this. Tamsen Donner, heroine that she was, kept a diary which would have been valuable for us, but this was lost along with her paintings and her botanical collections. The best preserved diary is that of Patrick Breen, done in simple and matter-of-fact fashion throughout most of the starving winter. Thus:

Dec. 17. Pleasant; William Murphy returned from the mountain party last evening; Baylis Williams died night before last; Milton and Noah started for Donner's eight days ago; not returned yet; think they are lost in the snow.

Dec. 21.   Milton got back last night from Donner's camp.   Sad news; Jacob Donner, Samuel Shoemaker, Rhineheart, and Smith are dead; the rest of them in a low situation; snowed all night, with a strong southwest wind.

Dec. 23.   Clear to-day; Milton took some of his meat away; all well at their camp.   Began this day to read the "Thirty Days' Prayers"; Almighty God, grant the requests of unworthy sinners!

Jan. 13.   Snowing fast; snow higher than the shanty; it must be thirteen feet deep.   Can not get wood this morning; it is a dreadful sight for us to look upon.

Jan. 27.   Commenced snowing yesterday; still continues today.   Lewis Keseberg, Jr., died three days ago; food growing scarce; don't have fire enough to cook our hides.

Jan. 31.   The sun does not shine out brilliant this morning; froze hard last night; wind northwest.   Landrum Murphy died last night about ten o'clock; Mrs. Reed went to Graves's this morning to look after goods.

Feb. 4.   Snowed hard until twelve o'clock last night; many uneasy for fear we shall all perish with hunger; we have but little meat left, and only three hides; Mrs. Reed has nothing but one hide, and that is on Graves's house; Milton lives there, and likely will keep that.   Eddy's child died last night.

Feb. 7.   Ceased to snow at last; today it is quite pleasant.   McCutchen's child died on the second of this month.

[This child died and was buried in the Graves's cabin. Mr. W. C. Graves helped dig the grave near one side of the cabin, and laid the little one to rest.   One of the most heart-rending features of this Donner tragedy is the number of infants that perished.   Mrs. Breen, Mrs. Pike, Mrs. Foster, Mrs. McCutchen, Mrs. Eddy, and Mrs. Graves each had nursing babes when the fatal camp was pitched at Donner Lake.]

Feb. 8.   Fine, clear morning.   Spitzer died last night, and we will bury him in the snow; Mrs. Eddy died on the night of the seventh.

Feb. 9.   Mrs. Pike's child all but dead; Milton is at Murphy's, not able to get out of bed; Mrs. Eddy and child buried today; wind southeast.

Feb. 10.   Beautiful morning; thawing in the sun; Milton Elliott died last night at Murphy's cabin, and Mrs. Reed went there this morning to see about his effects.   John Denton trying to borrow meat for Graves; had none to give; they had nothing but hides; all are entirely out of meat, but a little we have; our hides are nearly all eat up, but with God's help spring will soon smile upon us.

There was one survivor of the camp at Donner Lake, a man named Lewis Keseberg, of German descent.   That he was guilty of repeated cannibalism cannot be doubted.   It was in his cabin that, after losing all her loved ones, the heroic Tamsen Donner met her end.   Many thought he killed her for the one horrid purpose.[1]

---

[1] Many years later (1879) Keseberg declared under oath to C. F. McGlashan that he did not take her life.   See *History of the Donner Party*, pp. 212, 213.

Such then is the story of one of the great emigrant parties who started West on a hazard of new fortunes in the early days of the Oregon Trail. Happily there has been no parallel to the misadventures of this ill-fated caravan. It is difficult — without reading these bald and awful details — to realize the vast difference between that day and this. Today we may by the gentle stages of a pleasant railway journey arrive at Donner Lake. Little trace remains, nor does any kindly soul wish for more definite traces, of those awful scenes. Only a cross here and there with a legend, faint and becoming fainter every year, may be seen, marking the more prominent spots of the historic starving camp.

Up on the high mountain side, for the most part hid in the forest, lie the snowsheds and tunnels of the railway, now encountering its stiffest climb up the steep slopes to the summit of the Sierras. The author visited this spot of melancholy history in company with the vice-president of the great railway line which here swings up so steadily and easily over the Sierras. Bit by bit we checked out as best we might the fateful spots mentioned in the story of the Donner Party. A splendid motor highway runs by the lakeside now.

While we halted our own car there, a motor
car drove up from the westward — following that
practical automobile highway which now exists
from the plains of California across the Sierras
and east over precisely that trail where once the
weary feet of the oxen dragged the wagons of
the early emigrants. It was a small car of no
expensive type. It was loaded down with camping equipment until the wheels scarcely could be
seen. It carried five human occupants — an Iowa
farmer and his family. They had been out to
California for a season. Casually they had left
Los Angeles, had traveled north up the valleys of
California, east across the summit of the Sierras,
and were here now bound for Iowa over the old
emigrant trail!

We hailed this new traveler on the old trail.
I do not know whether or not he had any idea of
the early days of that great highway; I suspect
that he could tell only of its present motoring
possibilities. But his wheels were passing over
the marks left more than half a century ago by
the cracked felloes of the emigrant wagons going
west in search of homes. If we seek history, let
us ponder that chance pause of the eastbound
family, traveling by motor for pleasure, here by

the side of the graves of the travelers of another day, itself so briefly gone. What an epoch was spanned in the passing of that frontier!

CHAPTER VII

THE INDIAN WARS

IT might well be urged against the method employed in these pages that, although we undertook to speak of the last American frontier, all that we really thus far have done has been to describe a series of frontiers from the Missouri westward. In part this is true. But it was precisely in this large, loose, and irregular fashion that we actually arrived at our last frontier. Certainly our westbound civilization never advanced by any steady or regular process. It would be a singularly illuminating map — and one which I wish we might show — which would depict in different colors the great occupied areas of the West, with the earliest dates of their final and permanent occupation. Such a map as this would show us that the last frontier of America was overleaped and left behind not once but a score of times.

The land between the Missouri and the Rockies, along the Great Plains and the high foothills, was crossed over and forgotten by the men who were forging on into farther countries in search of lands where fortune was swift and easy. California, Oregon, all the early farming and timbering lands of the distant Northwest — these lay far beyond the Plains; and as we have noted, they were sought for, even before gold was dreamed of upon the Pacific Slope.

So here, somewhere between the Missouri and the Rockies, lay our last frontier, wavering, receding, advancing, gaining and losing, changing a little more every decade — and at last so rapidly changed as to be outworn and abolished in one swift decade all its own.

This unsettled land so long held in small repute by the early Americans, was, as we have pointed out, the buffalo-range and the country of the Horse Indians — the Plains tribes who lived upon the buffalo. For a long time it was this Indian population which held back the white settlements of Kansas, Nebraska, the Dakotas, Montana, Wyoming, Colorado. But as men began to work farther and farther westward in search of homes in Oregon, or in quest of gold in Cali-

fornia or Idaho or Montana, the Indian question
came to be a serious one.

To the Army, soon after the Civil War, fell the
task of exterminating, or at least evicting, the
savage tribes over all this unvalued and unknown
Middle West. This was a process not altogether
simple. For a considerable time the Indians
themselves were able to offer very effective resistance to the enterprise. They were accustomed
to living upon that country, and did not need
to bring in their own supplies; hence the Army
fought them at a certain disadvantage. In
sooth, the Army had to learn to become half
Indian before it could fight the Indians on anything like even terms. We seem not so much to
have coveted the lands in the first Indian-fighting
days; we fought rather for the trails than for the
soil. The Indians themselves had lived there all
their lives, had conquered their environment, and
were happy in it. They made a bitter fight; nor
are they to be blamed for doing so.

The greatest of our Indian wars have taken place
since our own Civil War; and perhaps the most
notable of all the battles are those which were
fought on the old cow range — in the land of our
last frontier. We do not lack abundant records

of this time of our history. Soon after the Civil War the railroads began edging out into the Plains. They brought, besides many new settlers, an abundance of chroniclers and historians and writers of hectic fiction or supposed fact. A multitude of books came out at this time of our history, most of which were accepted as truth. That was the time when we set up as Wild West heroes rough skin-clad hunters and so-called scouts, each of whom was allowed to tell his own story and to have it accepted at par. As a matter of fact, at about the time the Army had succeeded in subduing the last of the Indian tribes on the buffalo-range, the most of our Wild West history, at least so far as concerned the boldest adventure, was a thing of the past. It was easy to write of a past which every one now was too new, too ignorant, or too busy critically to remember.

Even as early as 1866, Colonel Marcy, an experienced army officer and Indian-fighter, took the attitude of writing about a vanishing phase of American life. In his *Army Life on the Border*, he says:

I have been persuaded by many friends that the contents of the book which is herewith presented to the public are not without value as records of a fast-vanish-

ing age, and as truthful sketches of men of various
races whose memory will shortly depend only on romance, unless some one who knew them shall undertake
to leave outlines of their peculiar characteristics. . . .
I am persuaded that excuse may be found in the simple
fact that all these peoples of my description — men,
conditions of life, races of aboriginal inhabitants and
adventurous hunters and pioneers — are passing away.
A few years more and the prairie will be transformed
into farms. The mountain ravines will be the abodes
of busy manufacturers, and the gigantic power of
American civilization will have taken possession of the
land from the great river of the West to the very shores
of the Pacific. . . . The world is fast filling up. I
trust I am not in error when I venture to place some
value, however small, on everything which goes to form
the truthful history of a condition of men incident to
the advances of civilization over the continent — a condition which forms peculiar types of character, breeds
remarkable developments of human nature — a condition also which can hardly again exist on this or any
other continent, and which has, therefore, a special
value in the sum of human history.

Such words as the foregoing bespeak a large
and dignified point of view. No one who follows
Marcy's pages can close them with anything but
respect and admiration. It is in books such as
this, then, that we may find something about the
last stages of the clearing of the frontier.

Even in Marcy's times the question of our

Government's Indian policy was a mooted one. He himself as an Army officer looked at the matter philosophically, but his estimate of conditions was exact. Long ago as he wrote, his conclusions were such as might have been given forty years later.

The limits of their accustomed range are rapidly contracting, and their means of subsistence undergoing a corresponding diminution. The white man is advancing with rapid strides upon all sides of them, and they are forced to give way to his encroachments. The time is not far distant when the buffalo will become extinct, and they will then be compelled to adopt some other mode of life than the chase for a subsistence. . . . No man will quietly submit to starvation when food is within his reach, and if he cannot obtain it honestly he will steal it or take it by force. If, therefore, we do not induce them to engage in agricultural avocations we shall in a few years have before us the alternative of exterminating them or fighting them perpetually. That they are destined ultimately to extinction does not in my mind admit of a doubt. For the reasons above mentioned it may at first be necessary for our government to assert its authority over them by a prompt and vigorous exercise of the military arm. . . . The tendency of the policy I have indicated will be to assemble these people in communities where they will be more readily controlled; and I predict from it the most gratifying results.

Another well-informed army officer, Colonel Richard Dodge, himself a hunter, a trailer, and a rider able to compete with the savages in their own fields, penetrated to the heart of the Indian problem when he wrote:

The conception of Indian character is almost impossible to a man who has passed the greater portion of his life surrounded by the influences of a cultivated, refined, and moral society. . . . The truth is simply too shocking, and the revolted mind takes refuge in disbelief as the less painful horn of the dilemma. As a first step toward an understanding of his character we must get at his standpoint of morality. As a child he is not brought up. . . . From the dawn of intelligence his own will is his law. There is no right and no wrong to him. . . . No dread of punishment restrains him from any act that boyish fun or fury may prompt. No lessons inculcating the beauty and sure reward of goodness or the hideousness and certain punishment of vice are ever wasted on him. The men by whom he is surrounded, and to whom he looks as models for his future life, are great and renowned just in proportion to their ferocity, to the scalps they have taken, or the thefts they have committed. His earliest boyish memory is probably a dance of rejoicing over the scalps of strangers, all of whom he is taught to regard as enemies. The lessons of his mother awaken only a desire to take his place as soon as possible in fight and foray. The instruction of his father is only such as is calculated to fit him best to act a prominent part in the chase, in theft, and in murder. . . . Virtue, morality, generosity, honor, are words not only absolutely without significance to him, but are not accurately translatable into any Indian language on the Plains.

These are sterner, less kindly, less philosophic words than Marcy's, but they keenly outline the duty of the Army on the frontier. We made treaties with the Indians and broke them. In turn men such as these ignorant savages might well be expected to break their treaties also; and they did. Unhappily our Indian policy at that time was one of mingled ferocity and wheedling. The Indians did not understand us any more than we did them. When we withdrew some of the old frontier posts from the old hunting-range, the action was construed by the tribesmen as an admission that we feared them, and they acted upon that idea. In one point of view they had right with them, for now we were moving out into the last of the great buffalo country. Their war was one of desperation, whereas ours was one of conquest, no better and no worse than all the wars of conquest by which the strong have taken the possessions of the weak.

Our Army at the close of the Civil War and at the beginning of the wars with the Plains tribes was in better condition than it has ever been since that day. It was made up of the soundest and best-seasoned soldiers that ever fought under our flag; and at that time it represented a greater proportion of our fighting strength than it ever has before or since. In 1860 the Regular Army, not counting the volunteer forces, was 16,000. In 1870 it was 37,000 — one soldier to each one thousand of our population.

Against this force, pioneers of the vaster advancing army of peaceful settlers now surging West, there was arrayed practically all the population of fighting tribes such as the Sioux, the two bands of the Cheyennes, the Piegans, the Assiniboines, the Arapahoes, the Kiowas, the Comanches, and the Apaches. These were the leaders of many other tribes in savage campaigns which set the land aflame from the Rio Grande to our northern line. The Sioux and Cheyennes were more especially the leaders, and they always did what they could to enlist the aid of the less warlike tribes such as the Crows, the Snakes, the Bannacks, the Utes — indeed all of the savage or semi-civilized tribes which had hung on the flanks of the traffic of the westbound trail.

The Sioux, then at the height of their power, were

distinguished by many warlike qualities. They fought hard and were quick to seize upon any signs of weakness in their enemies. When we, in the course of our Civil War, had withdrawn some of the upper posts, the Sioux edged in at once and pressed back the whites quite to the eastern confines of the Plains. When we were locked in the death grip of internecine war in 1862, they rose in one savage wave of rebellion of their own and massacred with the most horrible ferocity not less than six hundred and forty-four whites in Minnesota and South Dakota. When General Sibley went out among them on his later punitive campaign he had his hands full for many a long and weary day.

Events following the close of the Civil War did not mend matters in the Indian situation. The railroads had large land grants given to them along their lines, and they began to offer these lands for sale to settlers. Soldier scrip entitling the holder to locate on public lands now began to float about. Some of the engineers, even some of the laborers, upon the railroads, seeing how really feasible was the settlement of these Plains, began to edge out and to set up their homes, usually not far from the railway lines. All this increase in the numbers of the white population not only infuriated the Indians the more, but gave them the better chance to inflict damage upon our people. Our Army therefore became very little more than a vast body of police, and it was always afoot with the purpose of punishing these offending tribesmen, who knew nothing of the higher laws of war and who committed atrocities that have never been equalled in history; unless it be by one of the belligerents of the Great War in Europe, with whom we are at this writing engaged — once more in the interest of a sane and human civilization. The last great struggle for the occupation of the frontier was on. It involved the ownership of the last of our open lands; and hence may be called the war of our last frontier.

The settler who pushed West continued to be the man who shared his time between his rifle and his plough. The numerous buffalo were butchered with an endless avidity by the men who now appeared upon the range. As the great herds regularly migrated southward with each winter's snows, they were met by the settlers along the lower railway lines and in a brutal commerce were killed in thousands and in millions. The Indians saw this sudden and appalling shrinkage of their means of livelihood. It meant death to them. To their minds, especially when they thought we feared them, there was but one answer to all this — the whites must all be killed.

Red Cloud, Crazy Horse, Roman Nose, American Horse, Black Kettle — these were names of great Indian generals who proved their ability to fight. At times they brought into the open country, which as yet remained unoccupied by the great pastoral movement from the south, as many as five thousand mounted warriors in one body, and they were well armed and well supplied with ammunition. Those were the days when the Indian agents were carrying on their lists twice as many Indians as actually existed — and receiving twice as many supplies as really were issued to the tribes. The curse of politics was ours even at that time, and it cost us then, as now, unestimated millions of our nation's dearest treasures. As to the reservations which the Indians were urged to occupy, they left them when they liked. In the end, when they were beaten, all they were asked to do was to return to these reservations and be fed.

There were fought in the West from 1869 to 1875 more than two hundred pitched actions between the Army and the Indians. In most cases the white men were heavily outnumbered. The account which the Army gave of itself on scores of unremembered minor fields — which meant life or death to all engaged — would make one of the best pages of our history, could it be written today. The enlisted men of the frontier Army were riding and shooting men, able to live as the Indians did and able to beat them at their own game. They were led by Army officers whose type has never been improved upon in any later stage of our Army itself, or of any army in the world.

There are certain great battles which may at least receive notice, although it would be impossible to mention more than a few of the encounters of the great Indian wars on the buffalo-range at about the time of the buffalo's disappearance. The Fetterman Massacre in 1866, near Fort Phil Kearney, a post located at the edge of the Big Horn Mountains, was a blow which the Army never has forgotten. "In a place of fifty feet square lay the bodies of Colonel Fetterman, Captain Brown, and sixty-five enlisted men.

Each man was stripped naked and hacked and scalped, the skulls beaten in with war clubs and the bodies gashed with knives almost beyond recognition, with other ghastly mutilations that the civilized pen hesitates to record."

This tragedy brought the Indian problem before the country as never before. The hand of the Western rancher and trader was implacably against the tribesmen of the plains; the city-dweller of the East, with hazy notions of the Indian character, was disposed to urge lenient methods upon those responsible for governmental policy. While the Sioux and Cheyenne wars dragged on, Congress created, by act of July 20, 1867, a peace commission of four civilians and three army officers to deal with the hostile tribes. For more than a year, with scant sympathy from the military members, this commission endeavored to remove the causes of friction by amicable conference with the Indian chiefs. The attitude of the Army is reflected in a letter of General Sherman to his brother. "We have now selected and provided reservations for all, off the great roads. All who cling to their old hunting-grounds are hostile and will remain so till killed off. We will have a sort of predatory war for years—every now and then be shocked by the indiscriminate murder of travelers and settlers, but the country is so large, and the advantage of the Indians so great, that we cannot make a single war and end it. From the nature of things we must take chances and clean out Indians as we encounter them."

Segregation of the Indian tribes upon reservations seemed to the commission the only solution of the vexing problem. Various treaties were made and others were projected looking toward the removal of the tribesmen from the highways of continental travel. The result was misgiving and increased unrest among the Indians.

In midsummer of 1868 forays occurred at many points along the border of the Indian Territory. General Sheridan, who now commanded the Department of the Missouri, believed that a general war was imminent. He determined to teach the southern tribesmen a lesson they would not forget. In the dead of winter our troops marched against the Cheyennes, then in their encampments below the Kansas line. The Indians did not believe that white men could march in weather forty below zero, during which they themselves sat in their tepees around their fires;

but our cavalrymen did march in such weather, and under conditions such as our cavalry perhaps could not endure today. Among these troops was the Seventh Cavalry, Custer's Regiment, formed after the Civil War, and it was led by Lieutenant-Colonel George A. Custer himself, that gallant officer whose name was to go into further and more melancholy history of the Plains.

Custer marched until he got in touch with the trails of the Cheyennes, whom he knew to belong to Black Kettle's band. He did not at the time know that below them, in the same valley of the Washita, were also the winter encampments of the Kiowas, the Comanches, the Arapahoes, and even a few Apaches. He attacked at dawn of a bleak winter morning, November 27, 1868, after taking the precaution of surrounding the camp, and killed Black Kettle, and another chief, Little Rock, and over a hundred of their warriors. Many women and children also were killed in this attack. The result was one which sank deep into the Indian mind. They began to respect the men who could outmarch them and outlive them on the range. Surely, they thought, these were not the same men who had abandoned Forts Phil Kearney, C. F. Smith, and Reno. There had been some mistake about this matter. The Indians began to think it over. The result was a pacifying of all the country south of the Platte. The lower Indians began to come in and give themselves up to the reservation life.

One of the hardest of pitched battles ever fought with an Indian tribe occurred in September, 1868, on the Arickaree or South Fork of the Republican River, where General "Sandy" Forsyth, and his scouts, for nine days fought over six hundred Cheyennes and Arapahoes. These savages had been committing atrocities upon the settlers of the Saline, the Solomon, and the Republican valleys, and were known to have killed some sixty-four men and women at the time General Sheridan resolved to punish them. Forsyth had no chance to get a command of troops, but he was allowed to enlist fifty scouts, all "first-class, hardened frontiersmen," and with this body of fighting men he carried out the most dramatic battle perhaps ever waged on the Plains.

Forsyth ran into the trail of two or three large Indian villages, but none the less he followed on until he came to the valley of the South Fork. Here the Cheyennes under the redoubtable Roman Nose surrounded him on the 17th of September.

The small band of scouts took refuge on a brushy island some sixty yards from shore, and hastily dug themselves in under fire.

They stood at bay outnumbered ten to one, with small prospect of escape, for the little island offered no protection of itself, and was in point-blank range from the banks of the river. All their horses soon were shot down, and the men lay in the rifle pits with no hope of escape. Roman Nose, enraged at the resistance put up by Forsyth's men, led a band of some four hundred of his warriors in the most desperate charge that has been recorded in all our Indian fighting annals. It was rarely that the Indian would charge at all; but these tribesmen, stripped naked for the encounter, and led at first by that giant warrior, who came on shouting his defiance, charged in full view not only once but three times in one day, and got within a hundred feet of the foot of the island where the scouts were lying.

According to Forsyth's report, the Indians came on in regular ranks like the cavalry of the white men, more than four hundred strong. They were met by the fire of repeating car-bines and revolvers, and they stood for the first,

9

second, third, fourth, and fifth fire of repeating weapons, and still charged in! Roman Nose was killed at last within touch of the rifle pits against which he was leading his men. The second charge was less desperate, for the savages lost heart after the loss of their leader. The third one, delivered towards the evening of that same day, was desultory. By that time the bed of the shallow stream was well filled with fallen horses and dead warriors.

Forsyth ordered meat cut from the bodies of his dead horses and buried in the wet sand so that it might keep as long as possible. Lieutenant Beecher, his chief of scouts, was killed, as also were Surgeon Mooers, and Scouts Smith, Chalmers, Wilson, Farley, and Day. Seventeen others of the party were wounded, some severely. Forsyth himself was shot three times, once in the head. His left leg was broken below the knee, and his right thigh was ripped up by a rifle ball, which caused him extreme pain. Later he cut the bullet out of his own leg, and was relieved from some part of the pain. After his rescue, when his broken leg was set it did not suit him, and he had the leg broken twice in the hospital and reset until it knitted properly.

Forsyth's men lay under fire under a blazing sun in their holes on the sandbar for nine days. But the savages never dislodged them, and at last they made off, their women and children beating the death drums, and the entire village mourning the unreturning brave. On the second day of the fighting Forsyth had got out messengers at extreme risk, and at length the party was rescued by a detachment of the Tenth Cavalry. The Indians later said that they had in all over six hundred warriors in this fight. Their losses, though variously estimated, were undoubtedly heavy.

It was encounters such as this which gradually were teaching the Indians that they could not beat the white men, so that after a time they began to yield to the inevitable.

What is known as the Baker Massacre was the turning-point in the half-century of warfare with the Blackfeet, the savage tribe which had preyed upon the men of the fur trade in a long-continued series of robberies and murders. On January 22, 1870, Major E. M. Baker, led by half-breeds who knew the country, surprised the Piegans in their winter camp on the Marias River, just below the border. He, like Custer, attacked at dawn, opening the encounter with a general fire into the tepees. He killed a hundred and seventy-three of the Piegans, including very many women and children, as was unhappily the case so often in these surprise attacks. It was deplorable warfare. But it ended the resistance of the savage Blackfeet. They have been disposed for peace from that day to this.

The terrible revenge which the Sioux and Cheyennes took in the battle which annihilated Custer and his men on the Little Big Horn in the summer of 1876; the Homeric running fight made by Chief Joseph of the Nez Percés — a flight which baffled our best generals and their men for a hundred and ten days over more than fourteen hundred miles of wilderness — these are events so well known that it seems needless to do more than to refer to them. The Nez Percés in turn went down forever when Joseph came out and surrendered, saying, "From where the sun now stands I fight against the white man no more forever." His surrender to fate did not lack its dignity. Indeed, a mournful interest attached to the inevitable destiny of all these savage leaders, who, no doubt, according to their standards, were doing what men should do and all that men could do.

The main difficulty in administering full punishment to such bands was that after a defeat they scattered, so that they could not be overtaken in any detailed fashion. After the Custer fight many of the tribe went north of the Canadian line and remained there for some time. The writer himself has seen along the Qu'Appelle River in Saskatchewan some of the wheels taken out of the watches of Custer's men. The savages broke them up and used the wheels for jewelry. They even offered the Canadians for trade boots, hats, and clothing taken from the bodies of Custer's men.

The Modoc war against the warriors of Captain Jack in 1873 was waged in the lava beds of Oregon, and it had the distinction of being one of the first Indian wars to be well reported in the newspapers. We heard a great deal of the long and trying campaigns waged by the Army in revenge for the murder of General Canby in his council tent. We got small glory out of that war, perhaps, but at last we hanged the ringleader of the murderers; and the extreme Northwest remained free from that time on.

Far in the dry Southwest, where home-building man did not as yet essay a general occupation of the soil, the blood-thirsty Apache long waged a warfare which tried the mettle of our Army as perhaps no other tribes ever have done. The Spaniards had fought these Apaches for nearly three hundred years, and had not beaten them. They offered three hundred dollars each for Apache scalps, and took a certain number of them. But they left all the remaining braves sworn to an eternal enmity. The Apaches became mountain outlaws, whose blood-mad thirst for revenge never died. No tribe ever fought more bitterly. Hemmed in and surrounded, with no hope of escape, in some instances they perished literally to the last man. General George Crook finished the work of cleaning up the Apache outlaws only by use of the trailers of their own people who sided with the whites for pay. Without the Pima scouts he never could have run down the Apaches as he did. Perhaps these were the hardest of all the Plains Indians to find and to fight. But in 1872 Crook subdued them and concentrated them in reservations in Arizona. Ten years later, under Geronimo, a tribe of the Apaches broke loose and yielded to General Crook only after a prolonged war. Once again they raided New Mexico and Arizona in

1885–6. This was the last raid of Geronimo. He was forced by General Miles to surrender and, together with his chief warriors, was deported to Fort Pickens in Florida.

In all these savage pitched battles and bloody skirmishes, the surprises and murderous assaults all over the old range, there were hundreds of settlers killed, hundreds also of our army men, including some splendid officers. In the Custer fight alone, on the Little Big Horn, the Army lost Custer himself, thirteen commissioned officers, and two hundred and fifty-six enlisted men killed, with two officers and fifty-one men wounded; a total of three hundred and twenty-three killed and wounded in one battle. Custer had in his full column about seven hundred men. The number of the Indians has been variously estimated. They had perhaps five thousand men in their villages when they met Custer in this, the most historic and most ghastly battle of the Plains. It would be bootless to revive any of the old discussions regarding Custer and his rash courage. Whether in error or in wisdom, he died, and gallantly. He and his men helped clear the frontier for those who were to follow, and the task took its toll.

Thus, slowly but steadily, even though handicapped by a vacillating governmental policy regarding the Indians, we muddled through these great Indian wars of the frontier, our soldiers doing their work splendidly and uncomplainingly, such work as no other body of civilized troops has ever been asked to do or could have done if asked. At the close of the Civil War we ourselves were a nation of fighting men. We were fit and we were prepared. The average of our warlike qualities never has been so high as then. The frontier produced its own pathfinders, its own saviors, its own fighting men.

So now the frontier lay ready, waiting for the man with the plough. The dawn of that last day was at hand.

CHAPTER VIII

THE CATTLE KINGS

It is proper now to look back yet again over the scenes with which we hitherto have had to do. It is after the railways have come to the Plains. The Indians now are vanishing. The buffalo have not yet gone, but are soon to pass.

Until the closing days of the Civil War the northern range was a wide, open domain, the greatest ever offered for the use of a people. None claimed it then in fee; none wanted it in fee. The grasses and the sweet waters offered accessible and profitable chemistry for all men who had cows to range. The land laws still were vague and inexact in application, and each man could construe them much as he liked. The excellent homestead law of 1862, one of the few really good land laws that have been put on our national statute books, worked well enough so long as we had good farming lands for homesteading — lands of which a quarter section would support a home and a family. This same homestead law was the only one available for use on the cattle-range. In practice it was violated thousands of times — in fact, of necessity violated by any cattle man who wished to acquire sufficient range to run a considerable herd. Our great timber kings, our great cattle kings, made their fortunes out of their open contempt for the homestead law, which was designed to give all the people an even chance for a home and a farm. It made, and lost, America.

Swiftly enough, here and there along all the great waterways of the northern range, ranchers and their men filed claims on the water fronts. The dry land thus lay tributary to them. For the most part the open lands were held practically under squatter right; the first cowman in any valley usually had his rights respected, at least for a time. These were the days of the open range. Fences had not come, nor had farms been staked out.

From the South now appeared that tremendous and elemental force — most revolutionary of all the great changes we have noted in the swiftly changing West — the bringing in of thousands of horned kine along the northbound trails. The

trails were hurrying from the Rio Grande to the
upper plains of Texas and northward, along the
north and south line of the Frontier — that land
which now we have been seeking less to define
and to mark precisely than fundamentally to
understand.

The Indian wars had much to do with the
cow trade. The Indians were crowded upon the
reservations, and they had to be fed, and fed on
beef. Corrupt Indian agents made fortunes, and
the Beef Ring at Washington, one of the most
despicable lobbies which ever fattened there,
now wrote its brief and unworthy history. In a
strange way corrupt politics and corrupt business
affected the phases of the cattle industry as they
had affected our relations with the Indians. More
than once a herd of some thousand beeves driven
up from Texas on contract, and arriving late in
autumn, was not accepted on its arrival at the
army post — some pet of Washington perhaps had
his own herd to sell! All that could be done then
would be to seek out a " holding range."   In this
way, more and more, the capacity of the northern
Plains to nourish and improve cattle became established.

Naturally, the price of cows began to rise;

and naturally, also, the demand for open range steadily increased. There now began the whole complex story of leased lands and fenced lands. The frontier still was offering opportunity for the bold man to reap where he had not sown. Lands leased to the Indians of the civilized tribes began to cut large figure in the cow trade — as well as some figure in politics — until at length the thorny situation was handled by a firm hand at Washington. The methods of the East were swiftly overrunning those of the West. Politics and graft and pull, things hitherto unknown, soon wrote their hurrying story also over all this newly won region from which the rifle-smoke had scarcely yet cleared away.

But every herd which passed north for delivery of one sort or the other advanced the education of the cowman, whether of the northern or the southern ranges. Some of the southern men began to start feeding ranges in the North, retaining their breeding ranges in the South. The demand of the great upper range for cattle seemed for the time insatiable.

To the vision of the railroad builders a tremendous potential freightage now appeared. The railroad builders began to calculate that one day they would parallel the northbound cow trail with iron trails of their own and compete with nature for the carrying of this beef. The whole swift story of all that development, while the west-bound rails were crossing and criss-crossing the newly won frontier, scarce lasted twenty years. Presently we began to hear in the East of the Chisholm Trail and of the Western Trail which lay beyond it, and of many smaller and inter-mingling branches. We heard of Ogallalla, in Nebraska, the "Gomorrah of the Range," the first great upper market-place for distribution of cattle to the swiftly forming northern ranches. The names of new rivers came upon our maps; and beyond the first railroads we began to hear of the Yellowstone, the Powder, the Musselshell, the Tongue, the Big Horn, the Little Missouri.

The wild life, bold and carefree, coming up from the South now in a mighty surging wave, spread all over that new West which offered to the people of older lands a strange and fascinating interest. Every one on the range had money; every one was independent. Once more it seemed that man had been able to overleap the confin-ing limitations of his life, and to attain inde-pendence, self-indulgence, ease and liberty. A chorus of Homeric, riotous mirth, as of a land in laughter, rose up all over the great range. After all, it seemed that we had a new world left, a land not yet used. We still were young! The cry arose that there was land enough for all out West. And at first the trains of white-topped wagons rivaled the crowded coaches westbound on the rails.

In consequence there came an entire readjustment of values. This country, but yesterday barren and worthless, now was covered with gold, deeper than the gold of California or any of the old placers. New securities and new values appeared. Banks did not care much for the land as security — it was practically worthless without the cattle — but they would lend money on cattle at rates which did not then seem usurious. A new system of finance came into use. Side by side with the expansion of credits went the expansion of the cattle business. Literally in hundreds of thousands the cows came north from the exhaustless ranges of the lower country.

It was a wild, strange day. But withal it was the kindliest and most generous time, alike the most contented and the boldest time, in all the history of our frontiers. There never was a

better life than that of the cowman who had a
good range on the Plains and cattle enough to
stock his range. There never will be found a
better man's country in all the world than that
which ran from the Missouri up to the low foothills of the Rockies.

The lower cities took their tribute of the
northbound cattle for quite a time. Wichita,
Coffeyville, and other towns of lower Kansas in
turn made bids for prominence as cattle marts.
Agents of the Chicago stockyards would come
down along the trails into the Indian Nations to
meet the northbound herds and to try to divert
them to this or that market as a shipping-point.
The Kiowas and Comanches, not yet wholly con-
fined to their reservations, sometimes took tribute, whether in theft or in open extortion, of the
herds laboring upward through the long slow
season. Trail-cutters and herd-combers, licensed
or unlicensed hangers-on to the northbound
throngs of cattle, appeared along the lower trails
— with some reason, occasionally; for in a great
northbound herd there might be many cows
included under brands other than those of the
road brands registered for the drovers of that
particular herd. Cattle thieving became an in-

dustry of certain value, rivaling in some localities the operations of the bandits of the placer camps. There was great wealth suddenly to be seen. The weak and the lawless, as well as the strong and the unscrupulous, set out to reap after their own fashion where they had not sown. If a grave here or there appeared along the trail or at the edge of the straggling town, it mattered little. If the gamblers and the desperadoes of the cow towns such as Newton, Ellsworth, Abilene, Dodge, furnished a man for breakfast day after day, it mattered little, for plenty of men remained, as good or better. The life was large and careless, and bloodshed was but an incident.

During the early and unregulated days of the cattle industry, the frontier insisted on its own creed, its own standards. But all the time, coming out from the East, were scores and hundreds of men of exacter notions of trade and business. The enormous waste of the cattle range could not long endure. The toll taken by the thievery of the men who came to be called range-rustlers made an element of loss which could not long be sustained by thinking men. As the Vigilantes regulated things in the mining camps, so now in slightly different fashion the new property owners on the upper range established their own ideas, their own sense of proportion as to law and order. The cattle associations, the banding together of many owners of vast herds, for mutual protection and mutual gain were a natural and logical development. Outside of these there was for a time a highly efficient corps of cattle-range Vigilantes, who shot and hanged some scores of rustlers.

It was a frenzied life while it lasted — this lurid outburst, the last flare of the frontier. Such towns as Dodge and Ogallalla offered extraordinary phenomena of unrestraint. But fortunately into the worst of these capitals of license came the best men of the new régime, and the new officers of the law, the agents of the Vigilantes, the advance-guard of civilization now crowding on the heels of the wild men of the West. In time the lights of the dance-halls and the saloons and the gambling parlors went out one by one all along the frontier. By 1885 Dodge City, a famed capital of the cow trade, which will live as long as the history of that industry is known, resigned its eminence and declared that from where the sun then stood it would be a cow camp no more! The men of Dodge knew that

another day had dawned. But this was after
the homesteaders had arrived and put up their
wire fences, cutting off from the town the holding grounds of the northbound herds.

This innovation of barb-wire fences in the sev-
enties had caused a tremendous alteration of conditions over all the country. It had enabled men
to fence in their own water-fronts, their own homesteads. Casually, and at first without any ob-
jection filed by any one, they had included in
their fences many hundreds of thousands of acres
of range land to which they had no title whatever. These men — like the large-handed cow
barons of the Indian Nations, who had things
much as they willed in a little unnoted realm all
their own — had money and political influence.
And there seemed still range enough for all. If
a man wished to throw a drift fence here or
there, what mattered it?

Up to this time not much attention had been
paid to the Little Fellow, the man of small capital
who registered a brand of his own, and who —
with a Maverick[1] here and there and the natural

---

[1] In the early days a rancher by the name of Maverick, a Texas
man, had made himself rich simply by riding out on the open range
and branding loose and unmarked occupants of the free lands. Hence

increase, and perhaps a trifle of unnatural increase here and there — had proved able to accumulate with more or less rapidity a herd of his own.   Now the cattle associations passed rules that no foreman should be allowed to have or register a brand of his own.   Not that any foreman could be suspected — not at all! — but the foreman who insisted on his old right to own a running iron and a registered brand was politely asked to find his employment somewhere else. .

The large-handed and once generous methods of the old range now began to narrow themselves. Even if the Little Fellow were able to throw a fence around his own land, very often he did not have land enough to support his herd with profit. A certain antipathy now began to arise between the great cattle owners and the small ones, especially on the upper range, where some rather bitter wars were fought — the cow kings accusing their smaller rivals of rustling cows; the small men

the term "Maverick" was applied to any unbranded animal running loose on the range.   No one cared to interfere with these early activities in collecting unclaimed cattle.   Many a foundation for a great fortune was laid in precisely that way.   It was not until the more canny days in the North that Mavericks were regarded with jealous eyes.

accusing the larger operators of having for years done the same thing, and of having grown rich at it.

The cattle associations, thrifty and shifty, sending their brand inspectors as far east as the stockyards of Kansas City and Chicago, naturally had the whip hand of the smaller men. They employed detectives who regularly combed out the country in search of men who had loose ideas of mine and thine. All the time the cow game was becoming stricter and harder. Easterners brought on the East's idea of property, of low interest, sure returns, and good security. In short, there was set on once more — as there had been in every great movement across the entire West — the old contest between property rights and human independence in action. It was now once more the Frontier against the States, and the States were foredoomed to win.

The barb-wire fence, which was at first used extensively by the great operators, came at last to be the greatest friend of the Little Fellow on the range. The Little Fellow, who under the provisions of the homestead act began to push West and to depart farther and farther from the protecting lines of the railways, could locate land and water for himself and fence in both. "I've got the law back of me," was what he said; and what he said was true. Around the old cow camps of the trails, and around the young settlements which did not aspire to be called cow camps, the homesteaders fenced in land — so much land that there came to be no place near any of the shipping-points where a big herd from the South could be held. Along the southern range artificial barriers to the long drive began to be raised. It would be hard to say whether fear of Texas competition or of Texas cattle fever was the more powerful motive in the minds of ranchers in Colorado and Kansas. But the cattle quarantine laws of 1885 nearly broke up the long drive of that year. Men began to talk of fencing off the trails, and keeping the northbound herds within the fences — a thing obviously impossible.

The railroads soon rendered this discussion needless. Their agents went down to Texas and convinced the shippers that it would be cheaper and safer to put their cows on cattle trains and ship them directly to the ranges where they were to be delivered. And in time the rails running north and south across the Staked Plains into the heart of the lower range began to carry most of the cattle. So ended the old cattle trails.

What date shall we fix for the setting of the sun of that last frontier? Perhaps the year 1885 is as accurate as any — the time when the cattle trails practically ceased to bring north their vast tribute. But, in fact, there is no exact date for the passing of the frontier. Its decline set in on what day the first lank "nester" from the States outspanned his sun-burned team as he pulled up beside some sweet water on the rolling lands, somewhere in the West, and looked about him, and looked again at the land map held in his hand.

"I reckon this is our land, Mother," said he.

When he said that, he pronounced the doom of the old frontier.

CHAPTER IX

THE HOMESTEADER

His name was usually Nester or Little Fellow. It was the old story of the tortoise and the hare. The Little Fellow was from the first destined to win. His steady advance, now on this flank, now on that, just back of the vanguard pushing westward, had marked the end of all our earlier frontiers. The same story now was being written on the frontier of the Plains.

But in the passing of this last frontier the type of the land-seeking man, the type of the American, began to alter distinctly. The million dead of our cruel Civil War left a great gap in the American population which otherwise would have occupied the West and Northwest after the clearing away of the Indians. For three decades we had been receiving a strong and valuable immigration from the north of Europe. It was in great part this continuous immigration which occupied the farming lands of upper Iowa, Minnesota, and the Dakotas. Thus the population of the Northwest became largely foreign. Each German or Scandinavian who found himself prospering in this rich new country was himself an immigration agency. He sent back word to his friends and relatives in the Old World and these came to swell the steadily thickening population of the New.

We have seen that the enterprising cattlemen had not been slow to reach out for such resources as they might. Perhaps at one time between 1885 and 1890 there were over ten million acres of land illegally fenced in on the upper range by large cattle companies. This had been done without any color of law whatever; a man simply threw out his fences as far as he liked, and took in range enough to pasture all the cattle that he owned. His only pretext was "I saw it first." For the Nester who wanted a way through these fences out into the open public lands, he cherished a bitter resentment. And yet the Nester must in time win through, must eventually find the little piece of land which he was seeking.

The government at Washington was finally obliged to take action. In the summer of 1885, acting under authorization of Congress, President Cleveland ordered the removal of all illegal inclosures and forbade any person or association to prevent the peaceful occupation of the public land by homesteaders. The President had already cancelled the leases by which a great cattle company had occupied grazing lands in the Indian Territory. Yet, with even-handed justice he kept the land boomers also out of these coveted lands, until the Dawes Act of 1887 allotted the tribal lands to the Indians in severalty and threw open the remainder to the impatient homeseekers. Waiting thousands were ready at the Kansas line, eager for the starting gun which was to let loose a mad stampede of crazed human beings.

It always was contended by the cowman that these settlers coming in on the semi-arid range could not make a living there, that all they could do was legally to starve to death some good woman. True, many of them could not last out in the bitter combined fight with nature and the grasping conditions of commerce and transportation of that time. The western Canadian farmer of today is a cherished, almost a petted being. But no one ever showed any mercy to the American farmer who moved out West.

As always has been the case, a certain number of wagons might be seen passing back East, as well as the somewhat larger number steadily moving westward. There were lean years and dry years, hot years, yellow years here and there upon the range. The phrase written on one disheartened farmer's wagon top, "Going back to my wife's folks," became historic.

The railways were finding profit in carrying human beings out to the cow-range just as once they had in transporting cattle. Indeed, it did not take the wiser railroad men long to see that they could afford to set down a farmer, at almost no cost for transportation, in any part of the new West. He would after that be dependent upon the railroad in every way. The railroads deliberately devised the great land boom of 1886, which was more especially virulent in the State of Kansas. Many of the roads had lands of their own for sale, but what they wanted most was the traffic of the settlers. They knew the profit to be derived from the industry of a dense population raising products which must be shipped, and requiring imports which also must be shipped. One railroad even offered choice breeding-stock free on request. The same road, and others also, preached steadily the doctrine of diversified farming. In short, the railroads, in their own interests, did all they could to make prosperous the farms or ranches of the West. The usual Western homestead now was part ranch and part farm, although the term "ranch" continued for many years to cover all the meanings of the farm of whatever sort.

There appeared now in the new country yet another figure of the Western civilization, the land-boomer, with his irresponsible and unregulated statements in regard to the values of these Western lands. These men were not always desirable citizens, although of course no industry was more solid or more valuable than that of legitimate handling of the desirable lands. "Public spirit" became a phrase now well known in any one of scores of new towns springing up on the old cow-range, each of which laid claims to be the future metropolis of the world. In any one of these towns the main industry was that of selling lands or "real estate." During the Kansas boom of 1886 the land-boomers had their desks in the lobbies of banks, the windows of hardware stores — any place and every place offering room for a desk and chair.

Now also flourished apace the industry of mortgage loans. Eastern money began to flood the western Plains, attracted by the high rates of interest. In 1886 the customary banking interest in western Kansas was two per cent a month. It is easy to see that very soon such a state of affairs as this must collapse. The industry of selling town lots far out in the cornfields, and of buying unimproved subdivision property with borrowed money at usurious rates of interest, was one riding for its own fall.

None the less the Little Fellow kept on going out into the West. We did not change our land laws for his sake, and for a time he needed no sympathy. The homestead law in combination with the preëmption act and the tree claim act would enable a family to get hold of a very sizable tract of land. The foundations of many comfortable fortunes were laid in precisely this way by thrifty men who were willing to work and willing to wait.

It was not until 1917 that the old homestead law limiting the settler to a hundred and sixty acres of land was modified for the benefit of the

stock-raiser. The stock-raising homestead law, as
it is called, permits a man to make entry for not
more than six hundred and forty acres of unap-
propriated land which shall have been designated
by the Secretary of the Interior as "stock-raising
land." Cultivation of the land is not required,
but the holder is required to make "permanent
improvements" to the value of a dollar and
twenty-five cents an acre, and at least one-half of
these improvements must be made within three
years after the date of entry. In the old times
the question of proof in "proving up" was very
leniently considered. A man would stroll down to
the land office and swear solemnly that he had
lived the legal length of time on his homestead,
whereas perhaps he had never seen it or had
no more than ridden across it. Today matters
perhaps will be administered somewhat more
strictly; for of all those millions of acres of open
land once in the West there is almost none left
worth the holding for farm purposes.

Such dishonest practices were, however, indig-
nantly denied by those who fostered the irrigation
and dry-farming booms which made the last phase
of exploitation of the old range. A vast amount
of disaster was worked by the failure of number-

less irrigation companies, each of them offering lands to the settlers through the medium of most alluring advertising. In almost every case the engineers underestimated the cost of getting water on the land. Very often the amount of water available was not sufficient to irrigate the land which had been sold to settlers. In countless cases the district irrigation bonds — which were offered broadcast by Eastern banks to their small investors — were hardly worth the paper on which they were written. One after another these wildcat irrigation schemes, purporting to assure sudden wealth in apples, pears, celery, garden truck, cherries, small fruits, alfalfa, pecans, eucalyptus or catalpa trees — anything you liked — went to the wall. Sometimes whole communities became straitened by the collapse of these overblown enterprises. The recovery was slow, though usually the result of that recovery was a far healthier and more stable condition of society.

This whole question of irrigation and dry farming, this or that phase of the last scrambling, feverish settling on the last lands, was sorely wasteful of human enterprise and human happiness. It was much like the spawning rush of the salmon from the sea. Many perish. A few survive. Certainly there never was more cruel injustice done than that to the sober-minded Eastern farmers, some of them young men in search of cheaper homes, who sold out all they had in the East and went out to the dry country to farm under the ditch, or to take up that still more hazardous occupation — successful sometimes, though always hard and always risky — dry farming on the benches which cannot be reached with irrigating waters.

Strangely changed was all the face of the cattle range by these successive and startling innovations. The smoke of many little homes rose now, scattered over all that tremendous country from the Rockies to the edge of the short grass country, from Texas to the Canadian line. The cattle were not banished from the range, for each little farmer would probably have a few cows of his own; and in some fashion the great cowmen were managing to get in fee tracts of land sufficient for their purposes. There were land leases of all sorts which enabled the thrifty Westerner who knew the inside and out of local politics to pick up permanently considerable tracts of land. Some of these ranches held together as late as 1916; indeed, there are some such old-time holdings still existent in the West, although far more rare than formerly was the case.

Under all these conditions the price of land went up steadily. Land was taken eagerly which would have been refused with contempt a decade earlier. The parings and scraps and crumbs of the Old West now were fought for avidly.

The need of capital became more and more important in many of the great land operations. Even the government reclamation enterprises could not open lands to the settler on anything like the old homestead basis. The water right cost money — sometimes twenty-five or thirty dollars an acre; in some of the private reclamation enterprises, fifty dollars an acre, or even more. Very frequently when the Eastern farmer came out to settle on such a tract and to meet the hard, new, and expensive conditions of life in the semi-arid regions he found that he could not pay out on the land. Perhaps he brought two or three thousand dollars with him. It usually was the industrial mistake of the land-boomer to take from this intending settler practically all of his capital at the start. Naturally, when the new farmers were starved out and in one way or another had made other plans, the country itself went to pieces. That part of it was wisest which did not kill the goose of the golden egg. But be these things as they may be and as they were, the whole readjustment in agricultural values over the once measureless and valueless cow country was a stupendous and staggering thing.

Now appeared yet another agency of change. The high dry lands of many of the Rocky Mountain States had long been regarded covetously by an industry even more cordially disliked by the cattleman than the industry of farming. The sheepman began to raise his head and to plan certain things for himself in turn. Once the herder of sheep was a meek and lowly man, content to slink away when ordered. The writer himself in the dry Southwest once knew a flock of six thousand sheep to be rounded up and killed by the cattlemen of a range into which they had intruded. The herders went with the sheep. All over the range the feud between the sheepmen and the cowmen was bitter and implacable. The issues in those quarrels rarely got into the courts but were fought out on the ground. The old Wyoming dead-line of the cowmen against intruding bands of Green River sheep made a considerable amount of history which was never recorded.

The sheepmen at length began to succeed in their plans. Themselves not paying many taxes, not supporting the civilization of the country, not building the schools or roads or bridges, they none the less claimed the earth and the fullness thereof.

After the establishment of the great forest reserves, the sheepmen coveted the range thus included. It has been the governmental policy to sell range privileges in the forest reserves for sheep, on a per capita basis. Like privileges have been extended to cattlemen in certain of the reserves. Always the contact and the contest between the two industries of sheep and cows have remained. Of course the issue even in this ancient contest is foregone — as the cowman has had to raise his cows under fence, so ultimately must the sheepman also buy his range in fee and raise his product under fence.

The wandering bands of sheep belong nowhere. They ruin a country. It is a pathetic spectacle to see parts of the Old West in which sheep steadily have been ranged. They utterly destroy all the game; they even drive the fish out of the streams and cut the grasses and weeds down to the surface

of the earth. The denuded soil crumbles under
their countless hoofs, becomes dust, and blows
away. They leave a waste, a desert, an abomi-
nation.

There were yet other phases of change which
followed hard upon the heels of our soldiers after
they had completed their task of subjugating the
tribes of the buffalo Indians. After the homesteads
had been proved up in some of the Northwest-
ern States, such as Montana and the Dakotas,
large bodies of land were acquired by certain
capitalistic farmers. All this new land had been
proved to be exceedingly prolific of wheat, the
great new-land crop. The farmers of the Northwest had not yet learned that no country long
can thrive which depends upon a single crop.
But the once familiar figures of the bonanza
farms of the Northwest — the pictures of their
long lines of reapers or self-binders, twenty,
thirty, forty, or fifty machines, one after the
other, advancing through the golden grain — the
pictures of their innumerable stacks of wheat —
the figures of the vast mileage of their fencing
— the yet more stupendous figures of the outlay
required to operate these farms, and the splendid
totals of the receipts from such operations —

these at one time were familiar and proudly presented features of boom advertising in the upper portions of our black land belt, which lay just at the eastern edge of the old Plains.

There was to be repeated in this country something of the history of California. In the great valleys, such as the San Joaquin, the first interests were pastoral, and the cowmen found a vast realm which seemed to be theirs forever. There came to them, however, the bonanza wheat farmers, who flourished there about 1875 and through the next decade. Their highly specialized industry boasted that it could bake a loaf of bread out of a wheat field between the hours of sunrise and sunset. The outlay in stock and machinery on some of these bonanza ranches ran into enormous figures. But here, as in all new wheat countries, the productive power of the soil soon began to decrease. Little by little the number of bushels per acre lessened, until the bonanza farmer found himself with not half the product to sell which he had owned the first few years of his operations. In one California town at one time a bonanza farmer came in and covered three city blocks with farm machinery which he had turned over to the bank owning the mortgages on his

lands and plant.   He turned in also all his mules
and horses, and retired worse than broke from an
industry in which he had once made his hundreds
of thousands.   Something of this same story was
to follow in the Dakotas.   Presently we heard no
more of the bonanza wheat farms; and a little
later they were not.   The one-crop country is
never one of sound investing values; and a land
boom is something of which to beware — always
and always to beware.

The prairie had passed; the range had passed;
the illegal fences had passed; and presently the
cattle themselves were to pass — that is to say,
the great herds.   As recently as five years ago
(1912) it was my fortune to be in the town of
Belle Fourche, near the Black Hills — a region
long accustomed to vivid history, whether of
Indians, mines, or cows — at the time when the
last of the great herds of the old industry there-
abouts were breaking up; and to see, coming down
to the cattle chutes to be shipped to the Eastern stockyards, the last hundreds of the last great
Belle Fourche herd, which was once numbered
in thousands.   They came down out of the blue-
edged horizon, threading their way from upper
benches down across the dusty valley.   The dust

of their travel rose as it had twenty years earlier on the same old trail. But these were not the same cattle. There was not a longhorn among them; there has not been a longhorn on the range for many years. They were sleek, fat, well-fed animals, heavy and stocky, even of type, all either whitefaces or shorthorns. With them were some old-time cowmen, men grown gray in range work. Alongside the herds, after the ancient fashion of trailing cattle, rode cowboys who handled their charges with the same old skill. But even the cowboys had changed. These were without exception men from the East who had learned their trade here in the West. Here indeed was one of the last acts of the great drama of the Plains. To many an observer there it was a tragic thing. I saw many a cowman there the gravity on whose face had nothing to do with commercial loss. It was the Old West he mourned. I mourned with him.

Naturally the growth of the great stockyards of the Middle West had an effect upon all the cattle-producing country of the West, whether those cattle were bred in large or in small numbers. The dealers of the stockyards, let us say, gradually evolved a perfect understanding among themselves as to what cattle prices ought to be at the Eastern end of the rails. They have always pleaded poverty and explained the extremely small margin of profit under which they have operated. Of course, the repeated turn-over in their business has been an enormous thing; and their industry, since the invention of refrigerator cars and the shipment of dressed beef in tins, has been one which has extended to all the corners of the world. The great packers would rather talk of "by-products" than of these things. Always they have been poor, so very poor!

For a time the railroads east of the stockyard cities of Kansas City and Chicago divided up *pro rata* the dressed beef traffic. Investigation after investigation has been made of the methods of the stockyard firms, but thus far the law has not laid its hands successfully upon them. Naturally of late years the extremely high price of beef has made greater profit to the cattle raiser; but that man, receiving eight or ten cents a pound on the hoof, is not getting rich so fast as did his predecessor, who got half of it, because he is now obliged to feed hay and to enclose his range. Where once a half ton of hay might have been sufficient to tide a cow over the bad part of the winter, the Little Fellow who fences his own range of a few hundred acres is obliged to figure on two or three tons, for he must feed his herd on hay through the long months of the winter.

The ultimate consumer, of course, is the one who pays the freight and stands the cost of all this. Hence we have the swift growth of American discontent with living conditions. There is no longer land for free homes in America. This is no longer a land of opportunity. It is no longer a poor man's country. We have arrived all too swiftly upon the ways of the Old World. And today, in spite of our love of peace, we are in an Old World's war!

The insatiable demand of Americans for cheap lands assumed a certain international phase at the period lying between 1900 and 1913 or later — the years of the last great boom in Canadian lands. The Dominion Government, represented by shrewd and enterprising men able to handle large undertakings, saw with a certain satisfaction of its own the swift passing from the market of all the cheap lands of the United States. It was proved to the satisfaction of all that very large tracts of the Canadian plains also would raise wheat, quite as well as had the prairies of Mon-

tana or Dakota. The Canadian railroads, with
lands to sell, began to advertise the wheat industry in Alberta and Saskatchewan. The Canadian
Government went into the publicity business on
its own part. To a certain extent European immigration was encouraged, but the United States
really was the country most combed out for
settlers for these Canadian lands. As by magic,
millions of acres in western Canada were settled.

The young American farmers of our near Northwest were especially coveted as settlers, because
they knew how to farm these upper lands far
better than any Europeans, and because each of
them was able to bring a little capital of ready
money into Canada. The publicity campaign
waged by Canadians in our Western States in
one season took away more than a hundred and
fifty thousand good young farmers, resolved to
live under another flag. In one year the State
of Iowa lost over fifteen million dollars of money
withdrawn from bank deposits by farmers moving
across the line into Canada.

The story of these land rushes was much the
same there as it had been with us. Not all succeeded. The climatic conditions were far more
severe than any which we had endured, and if the

soil for a time in some regions seemed better than some of our poorest, at least there waited for the one-crop man the same future which had been discovered for similar methods within our own confines. But the great Canadian land booms, carefully fostered and well developed, offered a curious illustration of the tremendous pressure of all the populations of the world for land and yet more land.

In the year 1911 the writer saw, all through the Peace River Valley and even in the neighborhood of the Little Slave Lake, the advance-guard of wheat farmers crowding out even beyond the Canadian frontier in the covetous search for yet more cheap land. In 1912 I talked with a school teacher, who herself had homestead land in the Judith Basin of Montana — once sacred to cows — and who was calmly discussing the advisability of going up into the Peace River country to take up yet more homestead land under the regulations of the Dominion Government! In the year 1913 I saw an active business done in town lots at Fort McMurray, five hundred miles north of the last railroad of Alberta, on the ancient Athabasca waterway of the fur trade!

Who shall state the limit of all this expansion?

The farmer has ever found more and more land on which he could make a living; he is always taking land which his predecessor has scornfully refused. If presently there shall come the news that the land boomer has reached the mouth of the Mackenzie River — as long ago he reached certain portions of the Yukon and Tanana country — if it shall be said that men are now selling town lots under the Midnight Sun — what then? We are building a government railroad of our own almost within shadow of Mount McKinley in Alaska. There are steamboats on all these great sub-Arctic rivers. Perhaps, some day, a power boat may take us easily where I have stood, somewhat wearied, at that spot on the Little Bell tributary of the Porcupine, where a slab on a post said, "Portage Road to Ft. McPherson" — a "road" which is not even a trail, but which crosses the most northerly of all the passes of the Rockies, within a hundred miles of the Arctic Ocean.

Land, land, more land! It is the cry of the ages, more imperative and clamorous now than ever in the history of the world and only arrested for the time by the cataclysm of the Great War. The earth is well-nigh occupied now. Australia,

New Zealand, Canada, even Africa, are colonization grounds. What will be the story of the world at the end of the Great War none may predict. For the time there will be more land left in Europe; but, unbelievably soon, the Great War will have been forgotten; and then the march of the people will be resumed toward such frontiers of the world as yet may remain. Land, land, more land!

Always in America we have occupied the land as fast as it was feasible to do so. We have survived incredible hardships on the mining frontier, have lived through desperate social conditions in the cow country, have fought many of our bravest battles in the Indian country. Always it has been the frontier which has allured many of our boldest souls. And always, just back of the frontier, advancing, receding, crossing it this way and that, succeeding and failing, hoping and despairing — but steadily advancing in the net result — has come that portion of the population which builds homes and lives in them, and which is not content with a blanket for a bed and the sky for a roof above.

We had a frontier once. It was our most priceless possession. It has not been possible to eliminate from the blood of the American West, diluted though it has been by far less worthy strains, all the iron of the old home-bred frontiersmen. The frontier has been a lasting and ineradicable influence for the good of the United States. It was there we showed our fighting edge, our unconquerable resolution, our undying faith. There, for a time at least, we were Americans.

We had our frontier. We shall do ill indeed if we forget and abandon its strong lessons, its great hopes, its splendid human dreams.

BIBLIOGRAPHICAL NOTE

ANDY ADAMS, *The Log of a Cowboy*, 1903. *The Outlet*, 1905. Homely but excellently informing books done by a man rarely qualified for his task by long experience in the cattle business and on the trail. Nothing better exists than Adams's several books for the man who wishes trustworthy information on the early American cattle business.

GEORGE A. FORSYTH, *The Story of the Soldier*, 1900.

GEORGE BIRD GRINNELL, *The Story of the Indian*, 1895.

EMERSON HOUGH, *The Story of the Cowboy*, 1897.

CHARLES HOWARD SHINN, *The Story of the Mine*, 1901.

CY WARMAN, *The Story of the Railroad*, 1898. The foregoing books of Appleton's interesting series known as *The Story of the West* are valuable as containing much detailed information, done by contemporaries of wide experience.

FRANCIS PARKMAN, *The Oregon Trail*, 1901, with preface by the author to the edition of 1892. This is a reprint of the edition published in 1857 under the title *Prairie and Rocky Mountain Life*, or *The California and Oregon Trail*, and has always been held as a classic in the literature of the West. It holds a certain amount of information regarding life on the Plains at the middle of the last century.

The original title is more accurate than the more usual one *The Oregon Trail,* as the book itself is in no sense an exclusive study of that historic highway.

COLONEL R. B. MARCY, U. S. A., *Thirty Years of Army Life on the Border,* 1866. An admirable and very informing book done by an Army officer who was also a sportsman and a close observer of the conditions of the life about him. One of the standard books for any library of early Western literature.

EMERSON HOUGH, *The Story of the Outlaw,* 1907. A study of the Western desperado, with historical narratives of famous outlaws, stories of noted border movements, Vigilante activities, and armed conflicts on the border.

NATHANIEL PITT LANGFORD, *Vigilante Days and Ways,* 1893. A storehouse of information done in graphic anecdotal fashion of the scenes in the early mining camps of Idaho and Montana. Valuable as the work of a contemporary writer who took part in the scenes he describes.

JOHN C. VAN TRAMP, *Prairie and Rocky Mountain Adventures or Life in the West,* 1870. A study of the States and territorial regions of our Western empire, embracing history, statistics, and geography, with descriptions of the chief cities of the West. In large part a compilation of earlier Western literature.

SAMUEL BOWLES, *Our New West,* 1869. Records of travel between the Mississippi River and the Pacific Ocean, with details regarding scenery, agriculture, mines, business, social life, etc., including a full description of the Pacific States and studies of the "Mormons, Indians, and Chinese" at that time.

HIRAM MARTIN CHITTENDEN, *The American Fur Trade of the Far West*, 1902. The work of a distinguished Army officer. Done with the exact care of an Army engineer. An extraordinary collection of facts and a general view of the picturesque early industry of the fur trade, which did so much toward developing the American West. See also his *History of Steamboat Navigation on the Missouri River* (1903).

A. J. SOWELL, *Early Settlers and Indian Fighters of Southwest Texas*, 1900. A local book, but done with contemporary accuracy by a man who also studied the Texas Rangers and who was familiar with some of the earlier frontier characters of the Southwest.

The foregoing volumes are of course but a few among the many scores or hundreds which will have been read avidly by every man concerned with frontier life or with the expansion of the American people to the West. Space lacks for a fuller list, but the foregoing readings will serve to put upon the trail of wider information any one interested in these and kindred themes.

Let especial stress again be laid upon the preeminent value of books done by contemporaries, men who wrote, upon the ground, of things which they actually saw and actually understood. It is not always, or perhaps often, that these contemporary books achieve the place which they ought to have and hold.

INDEX

Abilene (Kan.), 36, 37, 144

Adams, Thomas, 63

Alder Gulch (Mont.), 63, 70

American Horse, Indian chief, 123

Apache Indians, 134–35

Ashley, W. H., General, 89

Austin, S. F., 19

Australia, survival of Saxon frontier in, 6–7

Baker, E. M., Major, 131

Baker Massacre, 131–32

Bannack (Mont.), 65–68

Belle Fourche (S. D.), 165

Benton, Fort, 16, 63

Bent's Fort, 17

Black Kettle, Indian chief, 123, 127

Bonneville, B. L. E., Captain, 89

Breen, Patrick, diary, 106; quoted, 106–08

Bridger, Fort (Utah), 63, 101

Brown, George, associate of Plummer, 76–77

California, attraction for settlers (1849), 15; attempt to take Texas cattle to, 35; discovery of gold (1849), 57; bonanza wheat farmers in, 164–65

Campbell, 89

Canada, Western land boom in, 168–72

Carson, Kit, 92

Carson (Nev.), 59, 60

Cattle industry in the West,
17–19, 20–25, 26–27, 31 *et seq.*, 138 *et seq.*

Chicago, cattle market in, 167

Chisholm Trail, 141

Clark, William, 11

Coffeyville (Kan.), 14°

Commerce on the Santa Fé Trail, 83–87

Cowboy, product of the West, 40–41; costume and outfit, 42–48; work of the round-up, 48–51; amusements, 51–54; personal characteristics, 54

Crawford, Hank, sheriff of miners' court, 67

Crazy Horse, Indian chief, 123

Crook, George, General, 134

Cumberlands, survival of the frontier in the, 4–6

Custer, G. A., Lieutenant-Colonel, 127, 132–33, 135–36

Dance, Walter, 64

Dawes Act (1887), 153

Dempsey, Robert, 63

Dodge, Richard, Colonel, quoted, 118–19

Dodge City (Kan.), 36, 144–45, 146

Dodge, Fort, 37

Donner, Tamsen, 98, 106–09; letter of, 98–101

Donner Party, 98–109

Ellsworth (Kan.), 36, 145

Fetterman Massacre, 124–26

Fisk, J. L., Captain, 64

Florence (Id.), 59, 63, 64

Forsyth, "Sandy," General, 128–131

Forty-Niners fail to discover wealth of Plains, 15

Fraser River valley (B. C.), rush for gold to, 57, 59

Frémont, J. C., 17, 89, 92–93

Frontier, meaning of term, 1–10; fascination of, 2–3; focus of the old, 82; changing of, 112–13; last, 113; end of (1885), 156; an influence for good, 173

Geronimo, Indian chief, 135

Glick, Dr., 67

Gold, influence of discovery upon settlement, 57 et seq.

Gold Creek (Mont.), gold discovered, 62–63

Golddigger, Tom, 63

Graves, F. W., 104

Great Bend (Kan.), 36, 37

Hall, Fort, 16

Hauser, S. T., 64

Helena (Mont.), 70, 82

Helm, Boone, associate of Plummer, 78

Hereford, Robert, 63

Homestead law (1862), 137–40, 156–57

Homesteaders, the, 151 et seq.

Hough, Emerson, *The Story of the Cowboy*, cited, 31 (note)

Idaho, gold camps in, 58; gold seekers in, 59; Territory of, organized (1863), 68–69

Illinois, Texas cattle driven to, 35

Indians, of the Plains, 14; use of horses by, 21; troubles in Montana, 70; conflicts with U. S. Army, 114 et seq.; segregation proposed, 126; as cattle thieves, 143–44

Irrigation, changes brought about by, 54; failure of many schemes, 157–60; Government reclamation enterprises, 160–61

Ives, George, associate of Plummer, 76–77

Jacobs, J. M., 63

Joseph, Indian chief, 132

Kansas, boom of 1886, 155–56

Kansas City, cattle market in, 167

Keseburg, Lewis, 108

Langford, N. P., *Vigilante Days and Ways*, quoted, 68, 70–72, 77 (note), 79–80

La Vérendrye, 21

Lewis, Meriwether, 11

Lewis and Clark expedition, 11–15, 85

Lewiston (Id.), 59, 60

Lisa, Manuel, 89

Little Big Horn, battle on the, 132–33

Little Rock, Indian chief, 127

Long Trail, the, of the cattle range, 31–35, 36, 37–38

Louisiana, cattle taken to, 35

McGlashan, C. F., *The History of the Donner Party*, 94; quoted, 95–97, 102–03, 103–04

McKnight, Baird, and Chambers party, 86

Magruder, Lloyd, 76

Marcy, R. B., Colonel, *Army Life on the Border*, quoted, 115–16, 117

Maverick, 146–47 (note)

Meeks, Jake, 63

Mexico, original cow country, 21; trading with, 87

Miles, N. A., General, 135

Mississippi Valley, settlement of, 12–13

Missouri River as a frontier pathway, 88–90

Modoc War, 133

Montana, gold discovered in (1852), 62; miners come to Gold Creek (1857), 62–63; first election in, 63–64; population of mining camps, 65–66; Territory of, formed (1864), 69; life in mining camps, 70 *et seq.*; Vigilantes in, 76 *et seq.*

Mormons, 15

Natchez Trace, 19
Nevada, Texas herds driven to, 35; gold camps in, 57, 59
Newton (Kan.), 36, 145
North America as the frontier, 3–4
Northwest, the, effect of immigration on, 152–53; wheat growing in, 163–65

Ogallalla (Neb.), 141, 145
Oregon, gold seekers in, 59
Oregon Trail, 90–93
Oro Fino (Id.), 59
Overland Trail, *see* Oregon Trail

Pike, Zebulon, Captain, 85, 86
Pike's Peak, rush for gold to (1859), 58; settlers in Montana from, 64
Plummer, Henry, 66–67, 69–70, 74–75, 76–78
Powell, J. W., 63
Prairies, delay in settlement of, 12–13

Ray, Ned, associate of Plummer, 78
Red Cloud, Indian chief, 123
Roman Nose, Indian chief, 123, 129, 130

Salmon River mines, Montana settlers bound for, 64, 65
Salt Lake, supply post at, 65
Santa Fé Trail, 83–84, 85, 86, 91
Sheep-raising, 162–64

Sheridan, P. H., General, 126
Sherman, W. T., General, quoted, 125–26
Sibley, H. H., General, 121
Sioux Indians, 120–21, 132
Slade, Joseph, 80–81
Stinson, Buck, associate of Plummer, 78
Stockraising homestead law (1917), 157
Stuart, Granville, 62, 64
Stuart, James, 62, 64
Sublette, 89

Texas, colonizing of, 19; cattle industry in, 20 *et seq.*
Transportation, early methods, 30; railroads across the range, 30–31; on the Santa Fé Trail, 83–84; railroads' part in settling the West, 154–55

Vigilantes, in Montana, 76 *et seq.*; of the cattle range, 145
Virginia City (Mont.), 70, 71, 72
Virginia City (Nev.), 79

Walla Walla (Wash.), 59, 60, 65
Washington, gold seekers in, 59
West, character of the Old American, 7–10; "The Great American Desert," 12; settlement of, 15 *et seq.*; development of the cattle industry, 17–19; climate, 25–26; underlying causes of settlement, 30 *et seq.*; mining camps, 61; Territories organized and States admitted, 69 (note); changes in, 81–82; beginnings of commerce, 83–87
Western Trail, 141
Wichita (Kan.), 36, 143
Williams, Bill, 92
Wyeth, Nathaniel, 89

Yager, Red, associate of Plummer, 76, 77